D1430044

The Biblical Seminar

18

COPING WITH TRANSIENCE

COPING WITH TRANSIENCE

Ecclesiastes on Brevity in Life

Daniel C. Fredericks

jॐt
1993
jsot press

Dedicated to those who are oppressed by any means,
and for whom the transience of circumstances,
or of life itself,
is the only hope they know.

'... they have no one to comfort them.'

Ecclesiastes 4.1

Published by JSOT Press
JSOT Press is an imprint of
Sheffield Academic Press Ltd
343 Fulwood Road
Sheffield S10 3BP
England

Typeset by Sheffield Academic Press
and
Printed on acid-free paper in Great Britain
by Cromwell Press
Melksham, Wiltshire

British Library Cataloguing in Publication Data

Fredericks, D.C.
    Coping with Transience: Ecclesiastes on
    Brevity in Life.—(Biblical Seminar
    Series, ISSN 0266-4984; No. 18)
    I. Title II. Series
    223

    ISBN 1-85075-358-X

CONTENTS

PREFACE

This volume is intended to be a topical commentary with a specific interest in discovering the message of Ecclesiastes through the eyes of its key word. This rereading, of course, is one that needs to be defended finally by one's linear reading of the text, with reference to the many exegetical aids available. Intricate discussions of exegetical controversies are to be pursued in the many thorough commentaries referred to in the footnotes and bibliography, though those that are critical will be surveyed to introduce the pertinent problems.

The RSV translation is relied on heavily and changed only when its presuppositions conflict directly with the new directions of this interpretation of Ecclesiastes.

Finally, sincere gratitude is extended to Ilona Duka and Margaret Root for their hours of painstaking typing, editing and indexing.

Daniel C. Fredericks

ABBREVIATIONS

AB	Anchor Bible
ATD	Das Alte Testament Deutsch
Bib	*Biblica*
BKAT	Biblischer Kommentar: Altes Testament
BT	*The Bible Translator*
BZAW	Beihefte zur *ZAW*
CBQ	*Catholic Biblical Quarterly*
ETL	*Ephemerides theologicae lovanienses*
ETR	*Etudes théologiques et religieuses*
HAR	*Hebrew Annual Review*
HAT	Handbuch zum Alten Testament
HKAT	Handkommentar zum Alten Testament
ICC	International Critical Commentary
Int	*Interpretation*
ITQ	*Irish Theological Quarterly*
JAAR	*Journal of the American Academy of Religion*
JBL	*Journal of Biblical Literature*
JEA	*Journal of Egyptian Archaeology*
JJS	*Journal of Jewish Studies*
JNES	*Journal of Near Eastern Studies*
JSOT	*Journal for the Study of the Old Testament*
JSOTSup	*Journal for the Study of the Old Testament*, Supplement Series
JSS	*Journal of Semitic Studies*
JTS	*Journal of Theological Studies*
KAT	Kommentar zum Alten Testament
NCB	New Century Bible
Or	*Orientalia*
Sef	*Sefarad*
SJT	*Scottish Journal of Theology*
TD	*Theology Digest*
TRu	*Theologische Rundschau*
TZ	*Theologische Zeitschrift*
VT	*Vetus Testamentum*
VTSup	*Vetus Testamentum*, Supplements
ZAW	*Zeitschrift für die alttestamentliche Wissenschaft*
ZTK	*Zeitschrift für Theologie und Kirche*

Chapter 1

EVERYTHING IS BREATH!

The dragon-fly leaves its shell
That its face might but glance at the sun.
Since the days of yore there has been no permanence.

Gilgamesh Epic[*]

Those who are sensitive to the broadest implications of a cursed world will find instant rapport with a man referred to in Ecclesiastes as Qoheleth,[1] for he too views the human condition sympathetically. Those, however, who have insulated themselves from the unsettling realities beyond their immediate sight by a selective awareness and screened sensitivities might avoid the book and its bold challenges to perhaps 'safe' yet incomplete reflections and superficial perspectives. Qoheleth may frustrate the simple, but he stimulates the wise with his comprehensive and sweeping conclusion, 'Breath of breaths, utter breath, all is breath'[2] (1.2; 12.8). But how inconvenient! The whole

---

[*] *ANET*, p. 92.

1.   See the commentaries for the various views of its meaning. Quite literally it means 'the assembler'. Presumably his assemblage refers to people whom he wished to address (though proverbs, or women, or his experiences have all been suggested as well), thus the frequent reference to him as 'the Preacher'. This is an obvious anachronism and I would prefer 'Convener' technically, and 'Speaker' more loosely. Having introduced him as Qoheleth, I will continue to call him by his Hebrew name, denoting the position he holds, following the advice of R. Gordis, 'The meaning seems to be speaker or assembler, but the word is best left untranslated' in *Koheleth —The Man and his World* (New York: Schocken Books, 3rd edn, 1968), p. 204.

2.   This over-arching statement serves two roles in the rhetorical development of Ecclesiastes. That it is *the* thesis of the book is doubtful since important conclusions are drawn from it that might be better candidates for that role. Therefore, at times it serves as a presupposition, e.g. 8.14, 15. However, it is obvious that, especially early in Qoheleth's speech, the phrase serves as a conclusion to his specific quest for

meaning of Ecclesiastes depends on this somewhat ambiguous metaphor, 'breath'. Here, in this closest example of a disciplined philosophical enquiry in the Bible, in the deepest of intellectual investigations of reality, we find its all-inclusive conclusions expressed *poetically*! After viewing the widely divergent understanding of Ecclesiastes, one cannot help but wish for a more definitive expression. Surely the beauty of Ecclesiastes owes much to the formal poetry found in the book and its artistic turns of phrases and uses of metaphor, but when this foundational premise is involved, a challenging riddle is presented that engages our curiosity from the start.

The Hebrew word behind 'breath' is *hevel*,[1] for which the etymology is probably onomatopoeic; that is, it is *aspirated* initially with 'h' and continued by the *spirant* 'v' sound, thus spoken by the exhalation of breath that the word itself denotes.[2] The pronunciation is itself a direct illustration of what the word means. The importance of this word is clear from both its multiple and clustered arrangement at the critical positions in the very beginning and very end of Qoheleth's excursus, and in its thirty instances in between where it appears as a constant refrain.[3] To understand this metaphor then is to understand the book; and to understand this book is to better understand the bibilical wisdom literature in its many manifestations.

A typical view of the message of Ecclesiastes and its role in the development of the wisdom genre in ancient Israel is that it reflects a theological 'crisis' by its sceptical and critical analysis of the world

wisdom and folly, e.g. 2.11. See G.S. Ogden, *Qoheleth* (Sheffield: JSOT Press, 1987), p. 14.

1.   Of course the exact orthography is *hebel* with the aspirated *beth*. The choice of spelling as *hevel* here and throughout this work is purely pragmatic and for English readers. For more information on this word's *literal* meaning, see e.g. BDB, pp. 210-11; K. Seybold, '*hebel*', TDOT, III, p. 315; O. Loretz, *Qohelet und der alte Orient* (Frieburg: Herder, 1964), pp. 218ff. The meaning of *hevel* as 'breath, vapor' is found outside biblical Hebrew only in Hebraized Aramaic dialects, e.g. Syriac, Mandean and southern Semitic.

2.   Seybold, '*hebel*', p. 314.

3.   1.2, 2, 2, 2, 2, 14; 2.1, 11, 15, 17, 19, 21, 23, 26; 3.19; 4.4, 7, 8, 16; 5.7, 10; 6.2, 4, 9, 11, 12; 7.6, 15; 8.10, 14, 14; 9.9, 9; 11.8, 10; 12.8, 8, 8. On the improbability that the reduction of the first vowel is an Aramaism (1.2, 2; 12.8) see D.C. Fredericks, *Qoheleth's Language: Re-evaluating its Nature and Date* (Lewiston, NY: Edwin Mellen, 1988), pp. 211-12, 220.

with conclusions contrary to an earlier, conventional and more optimistic wisdom presented in *Proverbs* and some wisdom psalms. For instance J.L. Crenshaw introduces his recent commentary on Ecclesiastes in this way:

> Life is profitless; totally absurd. This oppressive message lies at the heart of the Bible's strangest book. Enjoy life if you can, advises the author, for old age will soon overtake you. And even as you enjoy, know that the world is meaningless. Virtue does not bring reward. The deity stands distant, abandoning humanity to chance and death.
> These views contrast radically with earlier teachings expressed in the book of Proverbs.[1]

The book's composition is situated by most in the third century, when in reaction to Hellenism, the originator was stimulated to such free thinking; and according to some, was even led to refute or assimilate certain Greek ideas.[2] Ecclesiastes then is frequently seen as the logical conclusion, if not a main protagonist of a 'crisis' in Hebrew theology where scepticism led to an all-out cynicism, and where that cynicism in turn sees only inadequate justice everywhere, if any at all. For

---

1.   J.L. Crenshaw, *Ecclesiastes* (Philadelphia: Westminster Press, 1987), p. 23.

2.   Those of the nineteenth and early twentieth century who held to the Persian period as the background of Qoh's composition, include C.D. Ginsburg, *Coheleth, or the Book of Ecclesiastes* (London: Longman, 1861); S.R. Driver, *An Introduction to the Literature of the Old Testament* (Edinburgh: T. & T. Clark, 9th edn, 1913). However, the Greek age found more support, e.g. P. Haupt, *The Book of Ecclesiastes* (Baltimore: Johns Hopkins University Press, 1905); G.A. Barton, *The Book of Ecclesiastes* (ICC; Edinburgh: T. & T. Clark, 1908). By far the most consistent date given is that of the last half of the third century, e.g. W. Zimmerli, *Das Buch des Predigers Salomo* (ATD; Göttingen: Vandenhoeck & Ruprecht, 1862); Gordis, *Koheleth*; H.W. Hertzberg, *Der Prediger* (KAT; Gütersloh: Mohn, 1963); D. Lys, *L'Ecclésiaste ou que vaut la vie?* (Paris: Letouzey et Ané, 1977); A. Lauha, *Kohelet* (Neukirchen–Vluyn: Neukirchener Verlag, 1978); J.A. Loader, *Polar Structures in the Book of Qohelet* (BZAW, 152; Berlin: de Gruyter, 1979). There are those, however, who would suggest the latter fourth or early third centuries, e.g. Loretz, *Qohelet*; R.B.Y. Scott, *Proverbs, Ecclesiastes* (AB 18; Garden City, NY: Doubleday, 1965), and also those who have advocated or have been open to a second-century date, e.g. C.F. Whitley, *Koheleth: His Language and Date* (BZAW, 148; Berlin: de Gruyter, 1979); D.B. Macdonald, *The Hebrew Philosophical Genius* (Princeton: Princeton University Press, 1936). On the basis of a re-evaluation of Qoheleth's Hebrew it is quite possible that the date could be somewhat earlier than most would allow, see Fredericks, *Qoheleth's Language*. For a survey of the Greek influence theory, see likewise pp. 2-4.

Gordis, Qoheleth's 'quest for justice is as fruitless as the search for truth'.[1]

Beyond doubt, Qoheleth does emphasize the limitations of humanity's search for truth. Primarily those restrictions are either due to a person's finite life or finite mind. The first I will discuss at length in the next chapter. The second is a matter discussed by Qoheleth in all three tenses: humanity remembers little about the past (1.11; 2.16; 9.5, 15), it is not able to discover enough about the present (3.11; 7.14; 7.24; 8.17), nor able to predict much about the future (3.22; 6.12; 8.7; 9.1, 12; 10.14; 11.2, 5, 6). Furthermore, the sons of men by and large are not able to change the status quo whether determined by superiors (6.10; 8.4, 5), God himself (3.14; 7.13) or things in general (1.14). They meet their limit as well when attempting to tell of the weariness of life (1.8), when trying to sleep (2.23), trying to be creative in accomplishments (1.10; 2.12), attempting to enjoy life without God (2.25), to avoid sin (7.20), to restrain the wind (8.8), to demand justice (9.11) or remain strong (12.1-6). But the question remaining at this point is what over-all limitation is referred to by claiming that everything is breath? The reading of Ecclesiastes as 'crisis literature' is based on a certain pessimistic meaning of *hevel* in addition to these human confinements.

Of course any reading of Ecclesiastes is based on one's estimation of

---

1.   Gordis, *Koheleth*, p. 185. On the fatalism of Qoheleth see the following examples: O.S. Rankin, *Israel's Wisdom Literature* (New York: Schocken Books, 1969), p. 94; J.C. Rylaarsdam, *Revelation in Jewish Wisdom Literature* (Chicago: University of Chicago Press, 1946), pp. 25, 74; Zimmerli, 'The Place and Limit of the Wisdom in the Framework of the Old Testament Theology', *SJT* 17 (1964), pp. 156-57; H.H. Schmid, *Wesen und Geschichte der Weisheit* (Berlin: Töpelmann, 1966), pp. 192-93; G. von Rad, *Wisdom in Israel* (Nashville: Abingdon Press, 1972), pp. 265-65; M. Hengel, *Judaism and Hellenism* (Philadelphia: Fortress Press, 1974), p. 125; O. Kaiser, *Der Mensch unter dem Schicksal* (Berlin: de Gruyter, 1985), pp. 86-90. On the question of retribution and the act-consequence crisis in Qoheleth, see the following examples: Rankin, *Israel's Wisdom*, pp. 95-96; H. Gese, 'The Crisis of Wisdom in Koheleth', in J.L. Crenshaw (ed.), *Theodicy in the Old Testament* (Philadelphia: Fortress Press, 1983), pp. 141-53; R.E. Murphy, 'The Interpretation of Old Testament Wisdom Literature', *Int* 23 (1969), p. 299; K. Galling, *Der Prediger Salomo* (HKAT; Tübingen: Mohr, 1940), p. 79; E. Glasser, *Le procès du bonheur par Qohelet* (Lectio Divina, 61; Paris, 1970), pp. 199-200; Crenshaw, *Ecclesiastes*, pp. 24-28; F. Crüsemann, 'The Unchangeable World: The "Crisis of Wisdom" in Koheleth', in W. Schotroff and W. Stegemann (eds.), *God of the Lowly* (Maryknoll: Orbis Books, 1984), pp. 57-77.

this key word, and as it is used metaphorically in the book, it has
inevitably become a subject of controversy. Basically, there have been
two approaches to determine the meaning of 'breath' in Ecclesiastes:
the etymological, and the contextual. The persistent etymological
preference of translators and commentators has been along the lines of
'vanity, futility, emptiness', etc. In this century, however, other
meanings have been offered, encouraged by theories disposed to
contextual inductions rather than a pure etymological deduction. It is
fairly easy to trace the traditional understanding of *hevel* as 'vanity'.
The Septuagint translates *mataiótēs* for *hevel* in Ecclesiastes, a Greek
word denoting 'emptiness, futility, purposelessness, transitoriness'.[1]
The Vulgate, however, with *vanitas* ('emptiness') limited both the
richness and the options that inhere in the metaphor by precluding
the temporal meaning of 'transitoriness', leaving a meaning only
pertaining to value.[2] This connotation of valuelessness has taken
precedence ever since, and the translations seldom convey explicitly
the inherent transitoriness of *hevel*. For instance, both the AV and
RSV translate *hevel* as 'vanity' in each occurrence in Ecclesiastes. The
NEB renders it 'emptiness' in all but one case (5.7 'nothing', that is,
dreams and words). JB uses 'vanity' throughout except in 7.15 and 9.9
where life is said to be 'fleeting' in both instances.

Individual commentators have consistently and overwhelmingly
preferred the meaning of valuelessness as well. 'Vanity' is found
throughout G.A. Barton's commentary; Gordis alternates 'vanity' with
other words in only five passages. R.B.Y. Scott uses a number of variants in his less rigid translation; but all reflect the basic concept of
valuelessness. H.L. Ginsberg, A. Lauha, C.F. Whitley, O. Loretz, to
mention only a few others, also prefer the sense of valuelessness.[3]

Indeed 'vanity' is an appropriate rendering for most of the instances
of *hevel* outside Ecclesiastes in the Hebrew text. In many cultic

---

1. G. Bertram maps this development from the Hebrew realm of *hevel* to the
LXX in his 'Hebraischer und griechischer Qohelet', *ZAW* 64 (1952), pp. 26-49. That
the word connotes 'falsity, deceit' is denied by Bertram who sees this as a LXX
importation. Compare O. Bauernfeind, '*mataiótēs*', TDNT, IV, pp. 519-10; Gese,
Crisis of Wisdom, p. 150 n. 1; Whitley, *Koheleth*, pp. 172-73.
2. 'vanitas vanitatum dixit Ecclesiastes, vanitas vanitatum omnia vanitas.'
3. H.L. Ginsberg, 'The Structure and Contents of the Book of Koheleth',
VTSup 3 (1955), pp. 138ff.; Lauha, *Kohelet*, pp. 19, 30; Whitley, *Koheleth*, pp. 6-7;
Loretz, *Qohelet*, pp. 223, 299.

passages, idols are considered vain and valueless, hence *hevel*, e.g.
Deut. 32.21; 1 Kgs 16.13; Ps. 31.6; Jer. 8.19. In other cases one's
speech (Job 35.16) and wickedness (Jer. 2.5; 10.3) are unsubstantial
and *hevel*. However, where this is an unavoidable rendering in the
other texts, given their clearly negative message, this side of the
metaphor is unnatural in Ecclesiastes. Qoheleth emphasizes the *hevel*-
ness of *everything*.[1] Framed between his generalization that all is
breath in 1.2 and 12.8, are many commendations of joy and conventional wisdom which can only most cynically be pronounced 'empty'.
One purely logical but devastating move to solve this dilemma has
been to remove from the book all those statements recommending
wisdom.[2] By this Procrustean method, all such passages have been
appraised as inauthentic and as another's correction of an otherwise
all-too-cynical book. Yet the artificiality of this extreme excision of
substantial sections of Ecclesiastes has proven to most to be too
destructive.

Commentators have also tried to convey the *spirit* of *hevel*
with other words, e.g. 'bubble',[3] 'trace',[4] 'absurd',[5] 'ceaseless change'.[6]
And after struggling with its meaning, others prefer not to be
restricted by any hobgoblin of total consistency and opt for far more
creative renderings depending on the specific content and context that
is under consideration in each passage in Ecclesiastes.[7] For instance,

1.   The scope of 'all' (*hakkōl*) will be discussed in Chapter 6.

2.   Gordis conveniently cites examples of this process in regard to Eccl. 7.1-14,
Koheleth, p. 265. See Barton for an example of a list of excisions from throughout
Ecclesiastes; *Ecclesiastes*, pp. 43-46. Another approach is to generalize that Qoheleth
only quotes conventional wisdom to discount it significantly if not deny its truth.
This sweeping dismissal of classical wisdom from Qoheleth can not be sustained in
every, nor in the majority of cases. My third chapter will demonstrate this.

3.   F.C. Burkitt, 'Is Ecclesiastes a Translation?', *JTS* 22 (1921), pp. 27-28.

4.   L. Levy, *Das Buch Qoheleth* (Leipzig: Hinrichs, 1912), p. 12; R. Braun,
Kohelet und die frühhellenistische Popularphilosophie (BZAW, 130; Berlin: de
Gruyter, 1973), p. 45.

5.   A. Barucq, *Ecclésiaste* (Paris: Beauchesne, 1967), pp. 27-28; but not in the
existentialist meaning of 'absurd'.

6.   C.S. Knopf, 'The Optimism of Koheleth', *JBL* 49 (1930), p. 196; suppos-
edly Qoheleth's response to Heraclitus.

7.   T.J. Meek, 'Translating the Bible', *JBL* 79 (1960), p. 331. This is necessary
in the use of 'shadow' (*ṣēl*) in Ecclesiastes. It has three different connotations as a
metaphor: 6.12 uses it for its fleeting, fading, characteristic; 7.12 expresses
'protection' by the term; and 8.13 images a lengthened life by a lengthened shadow.

Gordis uses 'vanity', 'transitory' and 'folly' in different places; T.J. Meek suggests 'sorry', 'futility', 'empty', 'senseless' and 'transient'. But nearly all these variants still retain the skeptical side of *hevel*. Besides, as M.V. Fox has reasoned, given the standardization of the '*hevel*-judgments' it is expected that it have the same meaning in virtually all instances of its use.[1] It would become hopelessly obscure if one were to take the phrase 'everything is breath' and have any number of options for interpretation and translation in each context.

However, some have thought that the *entire* context of Ecclesiastes demands going outside of the predominant biblical etymology and searching for more appropriate definitions for Qoheleth's key word.[2] Fox himself induces 'absurd' from the word *hevel* in the type of extended study that this one word has long deserved,[3] likening Qoheleth's world-view to Albert Camus's existentialism voiced in his 'Myth of Sisyphus'.

> *Hebel* for Qoheleth, like 'absurd' for Camus, is not merely incongruous or ironic; it is oppressive, even tragic. The divorce between act and result is the reality upon which human reason founders; it robs human actions of significance and undermines morality. For Qoheleth *hebel* is an injustice, nearly synonymous with *rā'â*, inequity, injustice...As I see it, *hebel* designates...the manifestly irrational or meaningless.[4]

It is conceivable that we might have a modern existentialist interpretation of reality in the first millenium BCE, with all the despair and

1. M.V. Fox, 'The Meaning of *hebel* for Qohelet', *JBL* 105 (1986), pp. 413-14: 'The thematic declaration that everything is *hebel* and the formulaic character of the *hebel*-judgments imply that for Qohelet there is a single quality that is an attribute of the world and, further, that this quality is an attribute of the particular *habalîm* that Qohelet identifies by the formula "This too is a *hebel*". The *hebel* leitmotiv disintegrates if the word is assigned several different meanings. To do Qohelet justice, we must look for a concept appropriate to all, or, failing that, the great majority, of the specific *hebel*-judgments that are encompassed by the framing declaration of 1.2 and 12.8.'

2. E.g. E.M. Good, *Irony in the Old Testament* (Sheffield: Almond Press, 1981), p. 177: 'If etymology were the last word, we could as well translate the motto "a mere breath"...We must not assume the word's meaning beforehand, but need to see where and how Qoheleth uses it.' Good induces 'ironic' as *hevel*'s meaning. Ogden prefers 'enigmatic' by the same methodology (*Qoheleth*, pp. 17-18).

3. Fox, *Hebel*.

4. Fox, *Qohelet and his Contradictions* (JSOTSup, 71; Sheffield: JSOT Press, 1989), pp. 33, 34.

scorn of a literary Camus. It is conceivable that a profound mind like
that of Qoheleth is nevertheless fraught with significant theological
and philosophical contradictions. Perhaps though, we should not settle
too soon for such despairing attempts to explain the complexities of a
Qoheleth; rather perhaps there is a biblical meaning to *hebel*, contem-
porary with its composition, that would explain Qoheleth with greater
coherency.[1]

Other significant commentators have defined *hevel* more along
epistemological than metaphysical lines. W.E. Staples saw the word
to be connected with a cult and its presumed Moabite rain-god,
Hubal, and inferred that the mysterious essence of such a nature cult
was at the root of the Hebrew cognate, *hevel*, which then means
'incomprehensible'. This concept is not so foreign to Qoheleth's epistemological reservations that were outlined briefly above. But it is
doubtful whether one's limited knowledge is the most significant truth
Qoheleth wishes to emphasize.[2] Most recently, Ogden approaches
Ecclesiastes with just this understanding in his commentary, noting
Staples and Good before him.[3]

Etymology is surely not the last word in discovering the meaning of
words in any language; still, in the case of Ecclesiastes it may be
premature to neglect a viable and legitimate biblical meaning. One
other avenue has not been fully explored yet. Since a biblical meaning
of *hevel* is 'temporary', perhaps as its primary thrust in Ecclesiastes
our word connotes the transient aspect of reality.[4] Often when this

---

1.   It would have been interesting to see Fox interact more with Gordis's earlier
comparison of Qoheleth and existentialism. Gordis, *Koheleth*, pp. 112-21. See also
Schmid, *Wesen und Geschichte*, pp. 192ff.

2.   W.E. Staples, 'The "Vanity" of Ecclesiastes', *JNES* 2 (1943), pp. 95-104;
W.E. Staples, 'Vanity of Vanities', *Canadian Journal of Theology* 1 (1955),
pp. 141-56. Seybold (*hebel*, p. 318) responds negatively to this particular meaning,
and the similar opinions of others.

3.   Ogden, *Qoheleth*, p. 28.

4.   D.B. Macdonald most tantalizingly renders every *hevel* as 'transitory' in his
translation of Ecclesiastes. But no explanation is given for this consistent preference.
One can only assume that it is to be found in his juxtaposing of the eternality of God
and the ephemerality of man which he refers to only briefly. 'His philosophy was the
philosophy of a realist, of a man who, for himself, had looked steadily at life in all its
manifestations and who brought over nothing from the past save the one devastating
certainty that behind the passing phenomena of life there was an eternal and personal
Absolute, an unknowable Will and purpose' (*Philosophical Genius*, p. 87).

particular meaning has been applied to a passage in the book, it has been presumed that within the transience of something lies its inherent meaninglessness; so that, whether one starts with a meaning of *hevel* as 'vanity', or as 'temporary', the implication is the same: everything is futility, emptiness. The biblical evidence however does not present the word as always operating on this continuum, but often instead in contiguous spheres. Gordis has defined *hevel* in biblical Hebrew in this way:

> *Hebel* is 'breath, vapor'…breath is (a) unsubstantial, and (b) transitory. Hence from (a), *hebel* derives the meaning 'vanity' (Ecclesiastes *passim*; Ps. 94.11), from (b) the sense of 'short-lived'. This latter sense is to be found in Ps. 144:4, 'man is like breath', and should also be recognized in Job 7.16 'turn aside from me for my days are but a breath'.[1]

From a few passages in the Bible it is clear that transience is an appropriate connotation of *hevel*, free from any nuance of valuelessness.[2] As Gordis mentions above, Ps. 144.3, 4 does express this side of the word:

> O Lord, what is man that thou dost regard him,
> or the son of man that thou dost think of him?
> Man is like a breath
> his days are like a passing shadow.

The picture is that of brevity, the coming and going of the individual. That it does not speak of futility is clear from the up-beat tenor of the entire psalm, but most specifically by the immediate context. Verse 3 asks the very question which is answered from Psalm 8, man has a very substantial role of reigning over God's creation (Ps. 8.4-8). Here in Psalm 144, with the same phrasing, it would be improbable to hear the exact opposite, that humanity is of *no* importance. Instead we are left with an irony, not a contradiction—though humanity was created to rule, life is so brief!

The whole context of the three instances of *hevel* in Psalm 39 also proves it to have a separate meaning of 'transience' at times. It is clear enough apart from these three instances of *hevel*, that the psalmist is

---

1. Gordis, *Koheleth*, p. 205. Such a division is seen by others, e.g. Fox, 'It sometimes means "ephemeral", the sense most directly derivable from its literal meaning; for example, Prov. 21.6; Job 7.16; Pss. 39.6, 12; 144.4' (*hebel*, p. 412).
2. The source of Abel's name (*Hebel*) very possibly could be this aspect of transience, given the victim's destiny in Gen. 4. See Seybold, *hebel*, pp. 315-16.

counting on his temporary existence to relieve him from his agony.[1]
Verse 4 pleads,

> Lord let me know my end,
>> and what is the measure of my days;
>> let me know how fleeting (*ḥādēl*) my life is!

And v. 5 continues,

> Behold thou hast made my days a few handbreadths,
>> and my duration (*ḥeled*) is as nothing in thy sight.

Finally, v. 12 concludes metaphorically,

> For I am thy passing quest,
>> a sojourner, like all my fathers.

These verses help set the tone in which those phrases should be
understood where *hevel* does occur in the psalm (vv. 5, 6):

> Surely every man stands as a mere breath!
> Surely man goes about as a shadow.[2]
> Surely for *breath* they are in turmoil.
> Man heaps up and knows not who will gather![3]

And v. 11 reviews the transience of humanity,

> surely every man is a breath!

Here then is an entire psalm showing the brevity of life, aided by
expressions *denoting* brevity along with the *connotations* of *hevel*.

Rather than the brief lifespan of only the individual, another psalmist
ascribes brevity to the whole nation of Israel. Ps. 78.33 considers the
days of Israel to be shortened at God's sovereign discretion:

> So he made their days vanish like a breath
>> and their years in haste.[4]

Furthermore, and very relevant to Ecclesiastes, is that the same
impression is made a few verses further on (v. 39), where the nation
is linked to a *wind* (*rûaḥ*) that comes and goes quickly.

---

1.   P.C. Craigie, *Psalms 1–50* (Waco: Word Books, 1983), p. 307: 'Sickness
may be a part of the experience of age, but it is primarily the awareness of the near-
ness and inevitability of death that provokes [this] lament and prayer'.

2.   I will speak to the transience of a shadow below.

3.   A sentiment clearly in Qoheleth's mind (Eccl. 2.18-21, 26; 6.2).

4.   As *ḥdl* (fleeting) and *ḥld* (duration) in Ps. 39.4, 5 are word plays with
metathesized consonants, here *hbl* (breath) and *bhl* (haste) are plied in the same way.

He remembered that they were but flesh,
　　a wind that passes and comes not again.

It is precisely this parallel relationship between breath (*hevel*) and
wind (*rûaḥ*) that determines the constant refrain of Qoheleth, 'It is
breath and desire of the *wind*', a point we certainly need to return to
later.

It was seen above that the rhetorical question 'what is man?' plays
an occasional role in the poetry of Israel, for example, Psalms 8, 144.
It is found again in the context of *hevel*-ness in Job's bitter outburst in
ch. 7. Ironically, rather than seeing human significance as a blessing as
in Psalm 8, impertinent Job considers such attention from God to be a
curse, since God's attention was associated at this point with his pain
and suffering. Yet even this is not a statement of our futility, but an
affirmation of our value to God, which he would have gladly relin-
quished for the present (7.16, 17).

I loathe my life; I would *not live forever.*
　　Let me alone for *my days are breath.*
What is man that thou dost make so much of him
　　and that thou dost set thy mind upon him?

His hope is in his death, in his brevity, in his breath-like duration of
life; something he does not view as unique to himself, but true for all.
Later, he again emphasizes this brevity of life:

Man that is born of woman—short-lived (*gāṣēr*)
　　days, and full of trouble!

Furthermore, like Psalm 78 and Qoheleth, Job uses wind (*rûaḥ*) only a
few verses earlier to describe the brevity of existence, in the same
context that he has used breath (*hevel*).

My days are swifter than a weaver's shuttle,
　　and come to their end without hope [of deliverance].
Remember that *my life is wind* (*rûaḥ*)
　　my eye will never again see good (Job 7.6, 7).

Isaiah finds this parallel quite natural and helpful as well:

The wind (*rûaḥ*) will carry [the idols] off,
　　a breath (*hevel*) will take them away (57.13).

In yet another poetic book, *hevel* expresses transience; in Proverbs it
is advised,

> The getting of treasures by a lying tongue
> is a fleeting (*nidāp*) breath and a snare of death (21.6).[1]

And a related proverb warns,

> Wealth hastily (*hevel*) gotten will dwindle,
> but he who gathers little by little will increase it (13.11).[2]

It is clear enough then that, in the poetic corpus at least, *hevel* at times means 'temporary, fleeting' without any necessary linkage to the more desperate connotation that has been the preponderant interpretation and translation in Ecclesiastes.[3] Those cases of *hevel* outside of Ecclesiastes that are translated along the lines of 'temporary' are found primarily in poetic texts dealing with humanity and lifespan. It is especially then in the poetic/wisdom books that one should expect to see this special nuance. That a genre of literature can prefer certain words and meanings is well known, and it would be anticipated in Qoheleth and the other 'writings' too. For instance, Qoheleth's frequent use of 'toil' (*'āmāl*) is mirrored very disproportionately in the poetic books. It is also significant that at least four authors use the wind-breath duet to convey transience—an indication that it is a common poetic component used by many in the intellectual community for that purpose, including Qoheleth.

Qoheleth frequently speaks of the limits to human lifespan as well:

---

1.   For *hevel nidāp* as 'fleeting breath', see C.H. Toy, *The Book of Proverbs* (ICC; New York: Charles Scribner's Sons, 1902), p. 400; Scott, *Proverbs, Ecclesiastes*, pp. 123, 125. W. McKane takes *hebel* as 'vanity' here: *Proverbs: A New Approach* (Philadelphia: Westminster Press, 1975), pp. 243, 551-52.

2.   For *hevel* as the adverb, 'hastily', see Toy, *Proverbs*, p. 268; Again, McKane would differ, *Proverbs*, pp. 230, 458-59. The brevity of wealth is affirmed by Qoheleth as well, as we will see in Chapter 4 below.

3.   Two relevant psalm texts present a challenge to our thesis. Ps. 89.47, 48 connects brevity of life with literal 'emptiness' (*shāv'*). However, the statement does not use *hevel*, which is the word under study. Also, the text is not normative, but an embittered segment resolved predictably in the last line of the psalm. Ps. 62.9 elliptically says man is lighter than breath (*hevel*), yet it is the wicked of whom he is speaking, who *are* relatively insignificant in God's eyes.

One toils under the sun during the *few days*[1] of his life which God has given him, for this is his lot (5.18).

For who knows what is good for a man while he lives the *few days* of his *hevel* life, for he lives them as a shadow? (6.12).

Consequently, where both *hevel* and a person's lifespan is mentioned in Ecclesiastes, *hevel* could very well mean 'temporary' as it does elsewhere in the poetic/wisdom literature. Gordis represents many who see this thrust at least in 11.10 and the view of life's duration found there:

[hebel] here has its original meaning 'breath, vapor'...Hence our stich is to be rendered: 'for childhood and youth are a fleeting breath'. The same nuance is present in Ecclesiastes 6.12; 9.9.[2]

Furthermore, we will see in the next chapter that Qoheleth's pervasive concern about death and its implications for life is inextricably bound to this awareness of the brevity of life. It is more than possible that the whole issue of death in the book is not related primarily to any emptiness or vanity of life, but quite differently, to its impermanence.

Granted, the notion of brevities in life is evident to one degree or another in nearly every commentator's description of Qoheleth's message. However, a confusion results from mainly two methodological errors. One is to assume that transience in each case *implies* futility, emptiness, absurdity, which is certainly not necessary as we have seen through the other uses of *hevel*.[3] The other error is to see distinct spheres of meaning for the word and to select the correct one for each context, ending in a multifarious description of reality that is

1. That *mispār* means 'a small number' is standard lexicography (BDB, pp. 708-709). Even if one was to read simply 'the number of days', the term implies a limited, measured duration which ends in essentially the same idea; see Zimmerli, *Predigers*, p. 195, 'befristeten'; Lauha, *Kohelet*, p. 49, 'gezählten'. Though 'few days of his temporary life' may appear redundant, it is important to observe that Qoheleth defines that brevity in terms of *days*, not years, thus the qualification is significant. Furthermore, he continues this string of expressions for temporality in 6.12 by adding *ṣēl*.

2. *Koheleth*, p. 337. For further examples, see Glasser, *Qohelet,* p. 20; R.N. Whybray, 'Qoheleth, Preacher of Joy', *JSOT* (1982), p. 88.

3. Fox (*Hebel*, p. 441) argues correctly that, '*Hebel* does not include all of these senses in every application. The renderings suggested by the various translations and commentaries are not, it should be stressed, merely different nuances or colorations of one meaning, but distinct qualities: what is fleeting may be precious; what is frustrating may be no illusion; what is futile may endure forever.'

contrary to a significant purpose for the unifying and generalizing agenda of Qoheleth—'everything is breath'.[1] The question is, to what degree is transience not just an incidental or initial implication in Qoheleth's thought, but a major thread of the entire theme of the book? Is transience not really the singular emphasis of *hevel*? This is the challenge I would like to pursue. There are cases where *hevel* may connote 'futility', for example 5.7, 6.4, 11. But these are few and should not invert the proportion toward a message of futility for the book as a whole. It is as if Qoheleth assumes that we have learned that *life* is like a breath, brief in length; that fact we know from many poets and sages, not to speak of our own experience. But now he wants us to be aware of the fact that *every* experience within life is breath, everything will pass.

A key to this interpretation is found in the three main poems in his speech, 1.4-11, 3.1-8, 12.2-7. Each deals with transience and cyclicity. Early in Ecclesiastes, following the clustered phrase, 'brevities of brevities, brevity of brevities, all is brief', is a poem that speaks of the pattern in life that the clustered words themselves demonstrate in their own repetition. It continues the metaphor of transience and adds circularity to its description of reality. However, the poem only introduces what is obvious about breath itself, each breath is only one stage in the continuous cycle of breathing. It begins,

> A generation goes, and a generation comes,
>> but the earth remains forever.
> The sun rises and the sun goes down,
>> and hastens to the place where it rises.
> The wind blows to the south
>> and goes round to the north,

---

1.   We would then avoid aggregate definitions for Qoheleth's use of *hevel* which would be similar to Scott's, 'Thus the traditional translation "Vanities of vanities, all is vanity" can be freely expanded to read: "Everything in life is hollow and utterly futile; it is the thinnest of vapors, fleeting as a breath, and amounts to nothing"' (*Proverbs, Ecclesiastes*, p. 202); also M.A. Eaton, *Ecclesiastes* (Leicester: Inter-Varsity Press, 1983), p. 56: 'Ecclesiastes includes each of these emphases. All is untrustworthy, unsubstantial; no endeavour will in itself bring permanent satisfaction; the greatest of joys are fleeting'. For other examples of aggregate or selective definitions see Crenshaw, *Ecclesiastes*, e.g. pp. 58, 104, 131-32, 140; Zimmerli, *Predigers*, p. 144; Whybray, 'Joy', p. 88; Lys comes very close to emphasizing transience in *hevel*, but he ends with the convergence with 'sans valeur' (*L'Ecclésiaste*, p. 89).

round and round goes the wind,
　　and on its circuits the wind returns.
All streams run to the sea,
　　but the sea is not full;
to the place where the streams flow,
　　there they flow again (1.4-7).

This going and coming of generations is reminiscent of the 'passing' from life of Pss. 39.12 and 144.4, and repeated by Qoheleth himself in 3.20; 5.15, 16; 6.4. But this poem is not just about temporality but cyclicity as well.[1] Life is temporary, especially compared with the relative durability of the earth and its elements. A generation is temporary and generations are cyclical, yet even on this enduring earth the natural world swirls in rhythmic circuits. Qoheleth resumes this thought, even if for only a second in the third poem (12.2), 'the

---

1.　This poem has enjoyed much attention by scholars recently, particularly v. 4. A main issue discussed is whether 'generations' refers to human or natural circuits. Ogden ('The Interpretation of *dôr* in Ecclesiastes 1.4', *JSOT* 34 [1986]) argues that what others have thought referred to human generations actually refers to natural events; and Fox ('Qohelet 1.4', *JSOT* 40 [1988]) argues that what others have thought referred to the natural world (the earth) actually refers to the human population. An interesting exchange of ideas. Crenshaw believes it means both (*Ecclesiastes*, pp. 62, 63), and Whybray admits the positions are beyond proof ('Ecclesiastes 1.5-7 and the Wonders of Nature', *JSOT* 41 [1988], p. 107). Good takes these ambiguities in the poem to be intentional, to raise the emotional involvement (frustration) of the reader ('The Unfilled Sea: Style and Meaning in Ecclesiastes 1.2-11', in J.G. Gammie *et al.* [eds.], *Israelite Wisdom* [Missoula, MT: Scholars Press, 1978]). F. Rousseau surveys some views prior to his on this poem ('Structure de Qohelet I 4-11 et plan du livre', *VT* 31 [1981], p. 201). See also N. Lohfink, 'Die Wiederkehr des immer Gleichen: Eine fruhe Synthese zwischen griechischen und jüdischem Weltgefuhl in Kohelet 1, 4.11', *Archivio di Filosophia* 53 (1985), pp. 125-49. Whybray correctly discounts that futility is illustrated here, yet by interpreting 'generations' as natural cycles, he renders the poem less relevant to the book's obvious interest in human mortality. Given that the poem follows an allusion to human activity (1.3), and ends with a reference to a later generation (1.11d), given the predominant pairing of 'generations' and 'forever' in regard to human generations outside of Ecclesiastes, e.g. Exod. 3.15, Lev. 6.18, Pss. 33.11, 146.10, and given Qoheleth's own comments about future generations of people (1.11; 2.12, 18; 4.15), the verse is assumed to be talking about human transience. Thus Loader's view is preferred: 'For one who remembers that it is the same earth that is the stage for the repeated change from one generation to another, the emphasis on human volatility and transitoriness is heightened' (*Ecclesiastes* [Grand Rapids: Eerdmans, 1986], p. 20).

clouds return after the rain'. If there is longevity in anything, according to this poem, it is in its *repetition*, not in its individual duration. The generations are strung one after the other over the virtual eternality of the earth, upon which the 'wonderful and beneficial phenomenon' of the terrestrial elements follow themselves around (sunlight, wind, water). Nothing is new, yet everything is temporary.

For Qoheleth, the unity of reality is found in its repetition, not in eternal entities themselves (1.9-11; 2.12; 3.15; 6.10); a truth that he perhaps tries to mirror in the very structure of his entire speech. If any structural consistency lies in Ecclesiastes, it includes a cyclical consideration of matters, rather than an ever-developing, chronologically ordered argument.[1] As one 'progresses' through Ecclesiastes, there is nothing new, only repeated truths. As he peruses reality, Qoheleth breathes out and breathes in as one breathes the air, moving in directions from which he moves on, only to return to them again.[2] This is most evident in his repetitions of the 'this is breath' formula, as well as the 'nothing is better' pleas to enjoyment, themes that will be returned to in subsequent chapters of this study. Even at the very end, Qoheleth's summary of utter brevity follows the explicit cyclic return of the dust and the spirit of man (12.7, 8).

Qoheleth's second poem emphasizes human pursuits rather than natural cycles, yet describes them similarly in the manner of regular, seasonal events.

> For everything there is a season, and a time for every matter under
>   heaven:
> a time to be born, and a time to die;
> a time to plant, and a time to pluck up what is planted;

---

1. This is a point made quite recently by Whybray, *Ecclesiastes* (NCBC; Grand Rapids, Eerdmans, 1989), p. 17. For surveys of commentators' views on the structure or outline of the book, see C.D. Ginsburg's commentary which covers from apocryphal times to 1860 (*Coheleth*, pp. 27-243); Galling, 'Stand und Aufgabe der Kohelet Forschung', *TRu* 6 (1934), pp. 357-61; F. Ellermeier, *Qohelet* (Herzberg: Erwin Jungfer, 1967), pp. 129-40; A.G. Wright, 'The Riddle of the Sphinx: The Structure of the Book of Qoheleth', *CBQ* 30 (1968), pp. 314-20; Crenshaw, *Ecclesiastes*, pp. 34-49.

2. In three cases he literally 'looks again' (*šabtî 'anî* 4.1, 7; 9.11), and he reverts to his investigative posture after the first half of the book in 7.25 where his agenda is stated nearly identically to that in 1.17. On Qoheleth's penchant and purpose for the resumptive pronoun and the first person perfect, which most consider to be 'pleonastic', see Fredericks, *Qoheleth's Language*, pp. 62-82.

a time to kill, and a time to heal;
a time to break down, and a time to build up;
a time to weep, and a time to laugh;
a time to mourn, and a time to dance;
a time to cast away stones, and a time to gather stones;
a time to embrace, and a time to refrain from embracing;
a time to seek, and a time to lose;
a time to keep, and a time to cast away;
a time to rend, and a time to sew;
a time to keep silence, and a time to speak;
a time to love, and a time to hate;
a time for war, and a time for peace (3.1-8).

The two words for 'time' that introduce this poem, denote moments, or definitive segments of time, as opposed to indefinite durations,[1] expecially as they are set in direct opposition to eternity[2] that God instills in the hearts of humanity (3.11). Again, as in 1.4, eternality is the string upon which the alternate beads of human activity are strung.[3] To use Qoheleth's metaphor, the poem breathes rhythmically with metrical inhaling and exhaling. A time for this, a time for that. A

1.   This is certainly true for *zeman*. Whether *'ēt* does so inherently is a moot point. However, given that the stichs are in parallel form, that the subsequent poem emphasizes brevity, and that the uses of *'ēt* in Ecclesiastes have this sense, all suggest that both words carry the momentary meaning.
2.   Given the emphasis on time in this section of Qoheleth and the phrase 'from beginning to end', we prefer this meaning for *'ôlām*. Considering the endless debate this word has, and will continue to incite, one can only refer the reader to some discussions of the issue, e.g. E. Jenni, 'Das Wort *'ôlām* im alten Testament', *ZAW* 65 (1953), pp. 22-27; Whitley, *Koheleth*, pp. 31ff.; Ellermeier, *Qohelet*, pp. 302-22; Gordis, *Koheleth*, p. 231; J.L. Crenshaw, 'The Eternal Gospel', in J. Crenshaw and J. Willis (eds.), *Essays in Old Testament Ethics* (New York: Ktav, 1974); Loretz, *Qohelet*, pp. 281-85; Lys, *L'Ecclésiaste,* pp. 348-57; B. Isaksson, *Studies in the Language of Qoheleth* (Uppsala: Acta Universitatis Upsaliensis 1987), pp. 176-89.
3.   'If *ēt* and *zeman* speak of moments of time, then *'ôlām*, the new dimension of temporal awareness which God imparts, must refer to something in the time-spectrum lying beyond those moments, those extremities of time addressed in the poem.' Also, N. Lohfink, 'Oh, how effusively Qoheleth describes humanity's ever new and constantly vanishing moments! These moments are not vacuous: Every moment has content, be it good or evil... there is an eternal referent in each of our apparently irrevocably vanishing moments' ('The Present and Eternity: Time in Qoheleth', *TD* 34 [1987], pp. 237-39). This is the English popularization of 'Gegenwart und Ewigkeit: Die Zeit im Buch Kohelet', *Geist und Leben* 60 (1987), pp. 2-12.

time for this, a time for that. Inhale, exhale; inhale, exhale. The cadence
of polarity and opposition. The poem's very structure expresses the
'breathing' of life, breathing not the air, but breathing experiences
and their opposities in and out of reality. By this poem, Qoheleth
expands his metaphoric 'breath and the will of the wind' to a fuller
exposition of brevity and cyclicity. In fact, P. Haupt translated this
poem using transience as its fundamental thrust:

> All lasts but a while and transient
>   is everything under the sky:
> Transient are births and deaths,
>   transient are planting, uprooting.[1]

This same transience and cyclicity is addressed in 11.8–12.8, in regard
to the individual's brief life and return to his origins. But I will save
this exposition for Chapter 4.

It would be expected that other words or phrases denoting 'vanity'
would be found in Ecclestiastes apart from *hevel* if this were to be the
preferred hue of the word over 'temporary' or some equivalent.
Otherwise the case for the traditional meaning is considerably weaker
if *hevel*, itself the hub of the issue, is forced to carry the entire argument itself. However, those words that denote this more negative side
are totally absent, words that occur collectively nearly 100 times
outside of Ecclesiastes.[2]

'ayīn	(noun, 8 times) 'nothing, naught'; Pss. 39.6; 63.2; Isa. 40.17, 23; 41.11, 12, 24; Hag. 2.3
rêq	(adjective, 8 times) 'empty, idle, worthless'; Deut. 32.47; Judg. 9.4; 11.3; 2 Sam. 6.20; 2 Chron. 13.7; Ps. 4.3; Prov. 12.11; 28.19
rîq	(noun, 10 times) 'emptiness, vanity'; Lev. 26.16, 20; Job 39.16; Pss 2.1; 73.13; Isa. 30.7; 49.4; 65.23; Jer. 51.58; Hab. 2.13
šāw'	(noun, 52 times) 'emptiness, vanity'; e.g. Pss. 24.4; 60.13; 127.1, 1, 2
tōhû	(noun, 20 times) 'empty, unreal, worthless'; e.g. Isa. 29.21; 40.17, 23; 45.18, 19

1. Haupt, *Ecclesiastes*, pp. 12, 34.
2. An absence to which Lys alludes (*L'Ecclésiaste*, p. 88). Some might include
šeqer in this list, e.g. Seybold (*hebel*, p. 317), but that word's clear sense of 'deceit,
falsehood' is not an original sense of *hevel*. See p. 15 n. 1 above.

The absence of these words which Ecclesiastes could well have used to emphasize vanity or emptiness in life, if that was indeed a theme, suggests that this perhaps is not the main meaning of *hevel* for Qoheleth. One might suggest that Qoheleth intends *hevel* to carry all the weight itself. However, if the meaning of the very word is ambiguous enough, then its meaning actually depends substantially on the explicit view of life expressed in Ecclesiastes apart from the *hevel* passages. It would be quite unnatural for a writer to express the essence of his message only by one word or phrase throughout. One would expect expressions synonymous with a key word to surface at least here and there. If there is another biblical Hebrew meaning, and it is consistent with the rest of the ideas and expressions in the book, then it would be a more natural and preferred meaning of the metaphor. In light of Qoheleth's emphasis throughout his speech on life's ephemeral and circular destiny, perhaps transience should be adopted as the most appropriate, indeed, intended meaning for the word in most of its appearances.

Though the alternate words above are found nowhere in Ecclesiastes, there are companions of *hevel* that we do find attached to it in various phrases and could bear on its meaning. The most frequent phrase is 'desire of wind' (*rě'ût rûaḥ, ra'yôn rûaḥ*),[1] e.g. 1.14.

> I have seen everything that is done under the sun;
> and look, all is breath and the desire of wind.

The latter phrase is traditionally translated as 'vexation of spirit' (AV), 'striving after wind' (RSV), 'chasing the wind' (NEB), 'shepherding the wind',[2] and unfortunately occurs nowhere else in biblical Hebrew.

---

1. 1.14; 2.11, 17, 26; 4.4, 16; 6.9; Qoheleth's love for alliteration is evident in his formulaic *hevel* phrases (and is, incidentally the reason for our alliterated chapter titles). The summary statements in 1.2 and 12.8 are of course alliterated, *hăvēl hăvālîm, hăvēl hăvālîm hakkōl hăvēl*. But also *hinnēh hakkōl hěvēl* (1.14, 2.11), *hakkōl hăvēl* (2.17, 3.19), *hinnēh gam hû' hăvēl* (2.1), *gam-zeh hěvēl hû'* (2.23). Also, often in the same sentence as *hevel*, *ûrě'ût rûaḥ* (1.14; 2.11, 17, 26; 4.4, 6; 6.9), ra'yôn *rûaḥ* (1.17; 4.16), *rā'ā rabbā* (2.21).

2. E.g. Crenshaw, *Ecclesiastes*, pp. 68, 73. The options are due to different meanings of the root *rā'ā*: (1) to shepherd; (2) to associate with; (3) to desire (BDB, pp. 994-46), or, seeing *ra'a'* as the origin. Hos. 12.2 (Hebrew text) does join the words as *rō'eh rûaḥ*, but this one instance should not be *the* determining factor for Qoheleth's morphological and thematic (idiosyncratic) use. Presumably *rā'ā* (2) could also be a candidate for the meaning of this phrase. The evidence is too meager to be adamant either way. Though *rûaḥ* itself has 'breath' as its primary meaning in

Now these of course are consistent with the view that *hebel* means 'vanity'; surely chasing after the wind is futile. However, the phrase could be translated as a subjective, possessive genitive, as easily as the typical objective genitive. That is, it is as easily 'the wind's desire', as it is 'desiring the wind'.[1] This phrase then would be metaphorical just as *hevel* is, connoting the brevity of life and its experiences which are like the wind's desire that changes from north to south, east to west, downward, upward, around and even virtually still.

> The wind blows to the south,
> and goes round to the north;
> round and round goes the wind,
> and on its circuits the wind returns (1.6).

Yet this cyclicity of the wind is not the same as the wind's predictability, apart from its inevitable general patterns. In fact, Qoheleth speaks to the contrary in 11.5:

> As you do not know the way of the wind, nor how bones are formed in the womb of the pregnant women, so you do not know the work of God who makes everything.[2]

We have already emphasized how this same pairing of *hevel* (breath and *rûaḥ* (wind) appear in three other authors who wrote of brevity- Ps. 78.33, 39; Job 7.6, 7, 16-18; Isa. 57.13. Breath and wind strive together to convey how transient certain matters truely are. Yet another term is adopted along the way to express transience with breath and wind. 'Shadow' (*ṣēl*) is also interpreted to mean brevity within the genres and very books that we find the breath-wind pair (Ps. 102.12; 109.23; 144.4; Job 8.9; 14.2; 17.7; also 1 Chron. 29.15). And Qoheleth does parallel 'breath' with a 'shadow' for this purpose in 6.12:

biblical Hebrew, in these phrases in Ecclesiastes, 'wind' is most appropriate.

1. This is the flexibility of the construct-absolute syntax in Hebrew. The syntax suggested here is not innovative, it is that which Staples prefers 'striving of the *rûaḥ*', though he takes *rûaḥ*, to mean 'spirit'; 'Vanity of Vanities', p. 45. The obvious *objective* use is found in Eccl. 5.16, 'toil for wind (*lārûaḥ*)'. This is perhaps purposely distinguished morphologically from the more formulaic uses above.

2. Whether it is the way of the 'wind' or of the 'spirit' is uncertain given the frequent multi-feasible interpretation of *rûaḥ* in biblical Hebrew. Given the close connection of the wind and sowing in v. 4, and just as the wind here is again followed by sowing in v. 6, and since reading 'spirit' demands changing the consonantal text unnecessarily, we opt for 'wind', as do, e.g. Barton, *Ecclesiastes*, p. 183; Hertzberg, *Prediger*, pp. 199-200; Lauha, *Kohelet*, pp. 199, 202.

For who knows what is good for a man while he lives the few days of his
breath-like life, which he passes like a shadow?

In their interplay, these three metaphors suggest that the clause,
'breath and desire of wind', need not be rendered 'vanity and chasing
the wind', or some equivalent; instead they might be best translated,
'temporary and like the will of the wind'.

Three other companions of *hevel* occur but once each: 2.21 'a great
evil', 4.8 'an evil affliction', 6.2 'a sickening evil'. Each of these is a
description of a negative situation that was just recounted, but they are
awful circumstances regardless of the meaning of *hevel*. If anything,
they do not speak of a meaningless situation, but of a very significant
problem that at times only transience can remedy.

Finally, brevity in life is of course not a uniquely hebraic dis-
covery. Others of the ancient Near East experienced and sighed about
the same lamentable limitations as well. One ancient Egyptian from
the third millennium BCE was aware that 'life is a transitory state, and
even trees fall'.[1] The *Song of the Harper* refers to passing generations.
Other poetic literature also attests to the brevity of life and its
achievements.[2] I will refer to the relevant parallel extra-biblical
material in the following chapters, but for now it is sufficient to say
that to hear the same observations and their implications in the
Hebrew poetic scriptures, as in any culture's literature, is nothing less
than a fulfilled expectation.

Needless to say, the implications of reinterpreting *hevel* along the
lines of *transience* affects dramatically one's view of Ecclesiastes as a
whole. First, the book describes the human condition as being limited
in its duration and in the duration of its efforts, yet without emptying
life of true, though temporary value. Secondly, the book consoles
rather than disturbs the realist. It simultaneously reminds one of his
transience in this intimidating world with its pressing and tragic
problems, as well as comforts with the fact that evil itself is temporary in its impact on life. Transience of life then in addition to the

1.   'The Man who Was Tired of Life' dates to 2300–2100 BC. 'Transitory' is
R.O. Faulkner's translation of an Egyptian word denoting a limited amount, evi-
dently much like the function of *mispār* in Ecclesiastes; 'The Man who Was Tired of
Life', *JEA* 42 (1956), p. 27; see also R.J. Williams 'Reflections on the *Lebensmüde*',
JEA 48 (1962), p. 54.

2.   For brief summaries see Eaton, *Ecclesiastes*, pp. 33-36; Crenshaw,
Ecclesiastes, p. 51. For more detail see Loretz, *Qohelet*, pp. 83-134.

transience of all aspects of life carries its own contradiction, as a tortoise carries its blessed protection and cursed burden simultaneously. This realism is in line with at least one theme in the wisdom literature outside Ecclesiastes: how to cope in a world where wickedness and folly surrounds, and unfortunately outweighs, current righteousness and wisdom.[1] The advice of Qoheleth then is that true wisdom will recognize the temporality of virtually all that is experienced, and will accept the fact that our experience of a fallen world and the evil within is soon to pass.[2] Though it will lead to a substantially different interpretation of the book than it would if 'emptiness' is seen to be the thrust of *hevel*, it is consistent linguistically and contextually to prefer this temporal nuance of the word. Ecclesiastes profoundly and accurately presents to the reader the challenges involved in living in a world characterised by transitoriness, but not without adequate consolations and guidance on how to cope.

Though this reading of Ecclesiastes is significantly different from the current consensus on a 'crisis' reading, it is proposed in full understanding, and consequently, in rejection of just such a pessimistic reading. If Qoheleth is disenchanted with the human condition to the extent that for him everything is futile or absurd, then he is indeed naive and superficial to commend joy and wise behavior as often as he does. This picture of Qoheleth as a self-contradicting, incoherent thinker who concludes that life is both meaningless, yet an enjoyable gift of God, does not so much portray *his* thought as it does the despair of his interpreters in dealing with an admittedly linguistically and philosophically difficult text. It is the best of both worlds to maintain a legitimate biblical Hebrew connotation to *hevel* in most cases in the book, and to receive in return a more coherent, even though more conventional, Hebrew sage.

---

1. It is the same for Qoheleth as Craigie says of the psalmist's insights in Ps. 39, 'To combine an awareness of the transitory nature of the human life as a whole, with the wisdom that 'sufficient for the day is the evil thereof', is a starting point in achieving the sanity of a pilgrim in an otherwise mad world' (*Psalms 1–50*, p. 311).

2. Though naturally this reminder is appropriate for any generation, it is particularly germane to the youth, who are typically addressed by the biblical wisdom literature. Youth can view life as indefinitely long—death as simply a blur on the horizon. Who better would need the realistic instruction of one who had experienced the brevity of life and its components?

Chapter 2

BREVITY OF BREATH ITSELF

What is your life? For you are a vapor that appears for a little time and
then vanishes.

Jas 4.14

Whether death approaches us, or we feel it vicariously in the death of
another, it is the drone below all other counterpoints of life. We deal
with it in innumerable ways, from denying its inevitability, to actively
assisting its earliest arrival. We deal with it as the ultimate threat, the
ultimate relief, the ultimate meaning, the ultimate life, the ultimate
end, the ultimate beginning. Of course in his review of all events
under the sun, Qoheleth also is compelled to consider this subject as
well. In fact, death walks freely with Qoheleth, advising him
constantly along the way on his royal search for lasting profit.[1] The
speech begins with the passing of generations (1.4), ends with the
passing of the individual (12.1-7), and is perfectly bisected by verses
on the matter (6.12–7.4). Though indeed death is not *the* theme, it is
critical in its frequent contributions, emphasizing among other things,
the brevity of life itself. Ironically its importance to Qoheleth is not
that it has intimidated and terrified him dreadfully, but that it limits
life in so many ways that it cannot be ignored in such a comprehensive
investigation of life which Qoheleth intends to pursue. In fact, rather
than significant anxiety about death itself, he even commends it as
preferable to life at times (4.1-3; 7.1, 26)! Death then is not so much a
penetrating threat for him, as it is a fact, a necessary consideration in
one's contemplation of life. Actually it is *life* that can be the most

1.   See for instance, Crenshaw, 'The Shadow of Death in Qoheleth', in
J.G. Gammie (ed.), *Israelite Wisdom: Theological and Literary Essays in Honor of
Samuel Terrien* (Missoula, MT: Scholars Press, 1978).

formidable threat. Qoheleth is quite ambivalent about death; having resigned himself to the inevitable, he prefers to focus now on the implications of death on all that preceeds it—life cannot be understood apart from sober thinking about its end. The one who is truly serious about life will often reflect on the certainty of death, and Qoheleth describes the graphic choices to which reflection on death will lead:

> It is better to go to the house of mourning
>   than to go to a house of feasting;
> for this is the end to all men,
>   and the living take it to heart...
> The heart of the wise is in the house of mourning;
>   but the heart of fools is in the house of mirth (7.2, 4).

For Qoheleth a life busied and trivialized by superficial pursuits will not have the depth to observe and conclude the weighty ramifications of death on that life. P.C. Craigie says in reference to the poet of Psalm 39,

> By beginning to perceive clearly the transitory nature of human existence, the psalmist was also beginning to gain a broader perspective within which to interpret its difficulties and hardships; value in life and apprecia- tion of life must somehow be grasped within a full knowledge of its transitory nature.[1]

One might then see in the fact of death a blessing, as well as the curse. If death in all its severity as a school master forces one to live more authentically and lucidly, then it has imbued life with a value other- wise squandered by naivity. Admittedly, this is high tuition for the education acquired, but unfortunately (as in formal education) the only alternative is to settle for less than that for which we will surely pay.

Since conclusions on the value of life for Qoheleth are inextricable from death, Qoheleth takes his own advice and reflects thoroughly on mortality from many angles. First, he acknowledges that death is only one pole of our continuum of life. He often pairs one's origin and destiny to define more clearly the framing of life's duration.

> A time for birth, a time to die (3.2).

> All are from the dust, and all turn to dust again (3.20).

> As he came from his mother's womb he shall go again (5.15).

---

1.   Craigie, *Psalms 1–50*, p. 309.

Just as he came, so shall he go (5.16).
[The miscarriage] comes in transience and goes into darkness (6.4).

The day of death is better than the day of birth (7.1).

The dust returns to the earth as it was,
    and the breath returns to God who gave it (12.7).

Other verses dealing with origins are 4.2, 3; 4.14; 11.5. Qoheleth then is conscious of the full span of years found between these events, and assesses their value.

In his reflections on mortality he begins with the fundamentals. Death is inevitable, 'for the living know that they will die...' (9.5). Though he is highlighting the obvious, his wisdom still shows since there is no single most tragic truth that we more vigorously attempt to repress. The denial of death is not only a typical phase of the deceased's survivors, but was quite possibly the survival mode of the deceased before death.

As Qoheleth struggles with the certainty of death personally, he conveys his frustrations through emphasizing death's apparent indiscretions. The first annoying indiscretion on death's part is its claim on both the wise and the foolish. Qoheleth begins by offering a classical commendation of wisdom, but at the same time he remembers the leveling effect of death:

I saw that wisdom excels folly, as light excels darkness. The wise man has his eyes in his head, but the fool walks in darkness; and yet I perceived that one fate comes to both of them...How the wise man dies just like the fool (2.13, 14, 16b).

Death favours not the wise over the fool; at the end of the day it treats both equally and definitively. Death ultimately respects no one's efforts nor their inherent morality. It does not respect righteousness over unrighteousness. It is morally indifferent and cares as little for magnificent achievements as it does for good intentions.

It is the same for all. There is one fate for the righteous and for the wicked; for the good, for the clean, and for the unclean; for the man who offers a sacrifice and for the one who does not sacrifice. As the good man, so is the sinner; as the swearer is, so is the one who is afraid to swear. This is an evil in all that is done under the sun, that there is one fate for all men (9.2, 3a).

Even more ironic is death's apparent indiscretion in calling both beasts and humans; surely we deserve more of a future than a common animal! But in successive phrases the case for the equality of man and the beast is made tighter and tighter.

> For the fate of the sons of men and the fate of beasts is the same; as one dies so dies the other. They all have the same breath (*rûaḥ*),[1] and man has no advantage over the beasts; for all is temporary (*hevel*). All go to one place; all are from the dust, and all turn to dust again (3.19, 20).

Same fate, same death, same breath, same brevity, same origin, same destiny! How imprudent! Though Qoheleth is surely aware of the creation account of Genesis 2, and the superiority of man over land and beast (cf. Gen. 1.26-28), he is still aware that the same air is breathed, and the same physical elements are borne by both creatures.[2] However, by language reminiscent of Genesis 3 and the curse on Adam's race ('you are dust, and to dust you shall return'), we understand that this is not a fallacy in judgment on death's part, instead it is a result of God's judicial purposes. Having just referred to God's comprehensive judgment in 3.17,[3] Qoheleth tells us there is good reason behind this common fate of man and beast, 'God is testing them to show them that they are but beasts' (3.18). It is to prove to man that he is comparable to a beast, equally a creation of God equally subject to his will, and equally distant from the infinite transcendence of God, as the sun is essentially equidistant from all life on earth. Death's intention then is to humble humanity before that God. We might well transfer this very reason to the previous 'indiscretion' in death's claim upon the wise man and the fool—they are equally fools compared with the immeasurable and incomprehensible wisdom and righteousness of God. Certainly these equalizing functions of death for the wise, fools and beasts, are recognized by the Sons of Korah as well (Ps. 49.10, 12):

---

1. Here *rûaḥ* and *hevel* are paired yet again, but this time *rûaḥ* carries its primary meaning of 'breath'. Elsewhere when used in the context of *hevel*, it denoted the wind. See the first chapter of this volume.

2. See C.C. Forman's argument for Qoheleth's dependence on Genesis in his 'Koheleth's Use of Genesis' (*JSS* 5 [1960], pp. 256-63), germinated from a previous article of his, 'The Pessimism of Ecclesiastes', *JSS* 3 (1958), pp. 336-43. Also, Macdonald, *Philosophical Genius*, pp. 200-11.

3. The authenticity of 3.17 is questioned by some, but this matter will be discussed in Chapter 5.

Yes, he shall see that even the *wise* die,
    the *fool* and the stupid alike must perish
    and leave their wealth to others...
Man cannot abide in his pomp,
    he is like the *beasts* that perish.

To the wise, the fact of the *inevitability* of death is itself a consolation since it relieves us from the impossible task of devising ways
to avoid it. It emotionally and spiritually prepares the vigilant—we can
rest assured that an end is coming. Actually we have the whole course
of life's activities and events to remind us constantly that there is a
beginning and end to everything! The poem of 3.1-8 portrays all
activities and their times as measured events with only temporary
appropriateness. At the top of that list is 'a time for birth, a time to
die' (3.2). It is probable that here, in the wake of a discussion about
death and its implications for wisdom and skill (2.12-26), a consolation to death is in order. Considering death's position of priority in
that poem, it very probably becomes the object of it.[1]

Beyond the certainty of death however, Qoheleth gives a number of
consolations and means of coping with life's transience. First, though
life is indeed temporary, one's death is *timely*. He argues strongly
from the assumption of a sovereign, predetermining God who acts in
ways fully calculated, yet not calculable. Qoheleth is convinced that
God is entirely autonomous, free from any determinants, rendering
futile any exhaustive human prediction or mastery of reality. God
irreversibly ordains all events; 'whatever God does endures forever;
nothing can be added to it, nor anything taken from it' (3.14); 'who
can make straight what he has made crooked?' (7.13). God judges the
righteous and the wicked just as thoroughly, 'for he has appointed a
time for every matter, and for every work' (3.17).

Though timely from God's perspective, death is often a total sur-
prise. Though God has granted a specific number of days and years,
still,

> man does not know his time. Like fish which are taken in an evil net, and
> like birds which are caught up in a snare, so the sons of men are snared at
> an evil time, when it suddenly falls upon them (9.12).

1. 'The poem opens with life and death, which lie beyond human control.
Everything else in the list falls between these critical points' (Crenshaw, *Ecclesiastes*,
p. 93).

Since there is an appointed time to die (3.1, 2), no man has 'authority over the day of death' (8.8), neither over its sure arrival nor its schedule of arrival. As Ethan the psalmist wrote, 'What man can live and never see death? Who can deliver his soul from the power of Sheol?' (Ps. 89.48). It is in comparison with a normal lifespan then that 7.17 should be taken: 'Be not excessively wicked, neither be a fool; why should you die before your time?' Surely the sinner will not withdraw any days from his allotted life-time, but it might well appear to be a shorter life since an unexpected but justifiable end may come to a life of moral abandon (cf. Prov. 16.4).

For Qoheleth, the tension felt between impending tragedies and the assurance of God's timing of death is balanced from a realistic perspective grounded in orthodox Hebrew faith. A consolation to death and its indiscriminate attack on all, is that it submits to its master who allows it little slack on its leash, and who dictates its direction with relentless exactness. Death is even included in all those preordained events to which Qoheleth can ascribe beauty. 'God has made everything beautiful in its time' (3.11). Though he surely empathizes with others and their tragedies including death, still he is committed to the unquestionable goodness, the impeccable virtue of God. Though he can mourn most loudly, he believes most staunchly.

Qoheleth also observes that as inevitable and timely as death is from God's all-important perspective, there is always the hope of prolonging life by whatever means, whether by wisdom or by wickedness.[1] Classical wisdom spoke repeatedly about the benefits of wisdom including its life-preserving capability, so one should feel quite comfortable with Qoheleth's utilitarian views on the subject:

> Wisdom is good with an inheritance,
>   an advantage to those who see the sun.
> For the protection of wisdom is like the protection of money;
>   and the advantage of knowledge is that wisdom preserves the life of
>   him who has it (7.11, 12).
>
> Be not excessively wicked, neither be a fool; why should you die before
> your time? (7.17).

---

1.   Qoheleth asserts God's sovereignty and human responsibility just as ambivalently as theologians have before and ever since.

One is reminded of Proverbs's frequent advice, for example:

> The fear of the Lord prolongs life,
>   but the years of the wicked are short (10.27).[1]

Of course Qoheleth has his own examples of the protective value of wisdom that could avert death itself. Some are of benefit to the individual. For instance, one should take care when engaging in precarious duties like quarrying and logging (10.9-11), or when dealing with the potentially fatal whims of a king (8.2-6, 10.4, 20). Or the 'death' of a sovereign land can be prevented by wisdom applied against a foreign king (9.13-15), or exercised within the privy council (10.16, 17).

Though one can understand his cautions against excessive wickedness and folly (7.17) in order to prolong one's life, one can be stymied by the plea which precedes it, 'Be not excessively righteous, and do not be overly wise; why should you destroy yourself?'[2] However, this is not a window for moral license; it does not assume that restraining oneself from excessive righteousness necessarily entails *sinning* in the absence of that righteousness. That which is amoral can substitute for the exercise of righteousness and wisdom when the pursuit of these would end in the depletion of energy and options that might prove to be necessary for future endeavors. Doing all that one should, yet in less time than is physically and emotionally advisable, certainly will end in self-destruction. For example, one must sleep and eat to be productive for any significant length of time. To ignore these regularly for the pursuit of holiness is a needless fanaticism that does not impress Qoheleth. In fact, it flies right in the face of his theme of joy and pleasure. He is not condoning even a little wickedness, but is condemning an extremism that can turn righteousness and wisdom against themselves. The final editor of Ecclesiastes applies this to scholarship specifically:

> The sayings of the wise are like goads, and like nails firmly fixed are the collected sayings which are given by one shepherd. My son, beware of

---

1. Also Prov. 10.2, 16, 25; 11.4, 19, 30; 12.28; 13.9; 14.32; 19.16; etc.
2. This ticklish assertion has been turned in every direction to make it fit. We do not presume to lay the problem to rest here, but to propose a feasible interpretation and move on. See the commentaries in addition to Brindle, 'Righteousness and Wickedness in Ecclesiastes 7.15-18', *Andrews University Seminary Studies* 23 (1985), pp. 243-57; Whybray, 'Qoheleth the Immoralist? (Qoh 7.16-17)' in *Israelite Wisdom*, pp. 191-204.

anything beyond these. Of making many books there is no end, and much study is a weariness of the flesh (12.11, 12).

Since the body is so vulnerable to physical and mental stress, even wisdom can be too zealously striven after (a truth more often abused by those looking for an excuse than by those truly in danger of approaching life too seriously).

On the other hand, there are those who seek and apparently succeed in lengthening their lives, not by wisdom, but by wickedness; those seeking their own protection and for whom deferring to others in any noble gesture of self-sacrifice is seen to be the very worst strategy for their own success. A longer and more enjoyable life is possible for them only at the expense of others (4.1, 2; 8.9). Here an obtrusive image blurs the otherwise clear picture of how life should be preserved:

> I have seen everything in my fleeting days; there is a righteous man who perishes in his righteousness, and there is a wicked man who prolongs his life in his wickedness (7.15).

This observation disturbs a simpler generalization about justice and retribution where wisdom is rewarded and wickedness is cursed. Qoheleth certainly is aware of this disturbance since he has already recited the general rule only three verses earlier. But this is not a perspective peculiar to him; it is a well-known frustration for sensitive thinkers in any age, including those in the long history of the biblical Hebrews. Observations of this moral incongruity are heard in Jeremiah, Habakkuk, Malachi, Job and Psalms. If it is objected that the references outside Ecclesiastes have redeeming conclusions or implicit rebuttals, thus leaving Qoheleth alone in a moral cynicism, one need only read on. He too is sure that at the end of the day, justice prevails (I will look at this more thoroughly in a later chapter). Nonetheless, though life may be preserved by either wisdom or wickedness, it is only stalling the inevitable—the wise and the fool die alike!

However he does extend life in one other fashion—hypothetically. For Qoheleth life is so very fleeting, yet whether one is able to extend it by wisdom or wickedness, it is not the length that makes it more valuable. The value to life is found in one's enjoyment of life and in God's enjoyment of the individual. Theoretical extensions of life are used by Qoheleth to make these points. In order to highlight the

importance of satisfaction in life, an exaggerated lifespan is enter-
tained to show how a frustrated existence certainly is not improved by
longevity.

> If a man fathers a hundred children, and lives many years, so that the days
> of his years are many, but he does not enjoy good things, and also has no
> proper burial, I say that the miscarriage is better off than he (6.3).

Even if he were to live 2000 years, that person's perpetual dissatisfaction would make his situation more deplorable than that of the stillborn who had no post-natal life whatsoever. The conclusion? 'Even
though he should live a thousand years twice told, yet enjoy no
good—*do not all go to one place?*' (6.6). The unsatisfied person
eventually cannot even avoid the tragedy of the stillborn, instead, in
addition to his desperate life he must then experience that same fate as
well, whether his life has been long or short. And what of the
wicked's alleged extension of life by his sinfulness?

> Though a sinner does evil a hundred[1] times and prolongs[2] his life, still I
> know that it will be well for those who fear God, who fear him openly
> (8.12).

Any such 'lengthened' life will not find the sinner any better off than
the one with whom God is pleased. Instead, the apparently 'shorter'
life of the righteous will fare well.

Another consolation, better, obligation, in coping with life's transience is nothing less than a very theme of Ecclesiastes itself: Enjoy
life now! Though I will return to this at length in a subsequent
chapter, it should be at least introduced here as a significant balance to
the bitterness of death. In two passages dealing with life and death,
Qoheleth recommends joy in living. Eccl. 11.7–12.7 is clearly a unit
devoted to just this point—the certainty of death must not detract us
from current enjoyment and satisfaction. There he states and restates
that happiness in one's early life is not only desirable, but necessary if
there is to be substantial joy in life at all. Given the eventual days of
darkness, and since all in the future will be only perishable, given the
certainty of future vexations and pains, and the unrelenting decay of

---

1. It is perhaps only interesting that both of these conditionals about life
expectancy involve something amounting to *one hundred*: 100 children, 100 sins,
which are the only times the number is used in the book.
2. The sinner is found twice in Ecclesiastes trying to extend (*'ārak*) his life,
which even he feels is much too short (7.15, 8.12).

the body, Qoheleth still urgently and firmly advises extracting the joy from life while it still can be done.[1]

In 5.10–6.9, he deals with death and enjoyment as well. He begins with the maxim that a person leaves stripped of everything just as when he came.

> As he came from his mother's womb he shall go again, naked as he came, and shall take nothing for his toil, which he may carry away in his hand. This also is a grievous evil; just as he came, so shall he go (5.15, 16a).

As we have seen, even if that life were fictionally lengthened for the purpose of argument, if happiness is not in its destiny, then it would have been better to have never continued beyond birth (6.3-5). The entire unit of 5.10–6.9 gives numerous reasons for misery and dissatisfaction: disillusionment with riches (5.10), increased drains on personal resources (5.11), anxiety over riches (5.12), riches lost by some calamity (5.14), toiling for the wind (5.16), eating in darkness, with suffering, sickness and bitterness (5.17), seeing someone else enjoy one's own portion (6.1, 2). The cumulative force of these sources of discontent lead Qoheleth to commend the stillborn's state over the wretched life of the sorely burdened. On the other hand, a life of contentment is the implied consolation to death, a life aloof from any such comparison with the morbid state of the miscarriage. In two separate question/answer sequences, both introduced by 'what profit', the answer is to enjoy one's property as much and for as long as possible.

> What advantage is there for the owner but for his eyes to enjoy [his property] (5.11).

---

1. 'Thus he taught that, in youth, the recognition that old age was immanent and life was finite should become the impetus to motivate one's quest for happiness. For true joy was the means by which humanity could recognize the greatness of God: the more one enjoyed the goodness of life the more one appreciated the goodness of God. It is through Qoheleth's teaching that awareness of the limiting characteristics of life brings one to more fully appreciate the beauty in life, the joy of living in the present, and thereby the closeness one can feel with the Creator himself' (R.Z. Dulin, *A Crown of Glory: A Biblical View of Aging* [Ramsey, NJ: Paulist Press], pp. 46-47). Dulin's view reminds one of the *Westminster Shorter Catechism*, where it is said that humanity's 'chief end is to glorify God, and to enjoy him for ever'.

What profit has the wise man over the fool?...Better is the enjoyment[1] of
the eyes than the wandering of the soul (6.8, 9).

A clear implication of 5.10–6.9 is that a life of joy, though sure to
end, is a solace to one's apprehensions about death. In this passage the
pleasures are simple: pleasant sleep (5.12), eating, drinking and
enjoying one's work (5.18, 19). If these simple pleasures are adequate
to some extent to deaden the sting of death, certainly additional
blessings could only help numb it further.

Now *in light* of the pleasures of eating, drinking, fine appearance,
and marriage (9.7-9), yet *in spite* of both the pervasive perversity of
the human race (9.3) and the identical fatal end to the wicked and
wise, it is true that 'he who is joined with all the living has hope, for a
living dog is better than a dead lion' (9.4). Qoheleth offers these realistic observations and encouragements for those whose lives are not
absolutely unbearable. But it is equally true that there are circumstances which would lead to the opposite conclusion. The point of
Qoheleth's poem and commentary in 3.1-22 is that death, like birth,
war and love has its role to play in God's elaborate and often enigmatic script. But if death itself can mean relief, appearing at the most
beautiful moment, it is not so shocking, and surely not cynical, to hear
of its preference over life.

> A good name is better than precious ointment;
> and the day of death than the day of birth (7.1).

Qoheleth's conclusion is a throwback to the ancient Egyptian text,
'The Man who Was Tired of Life', from the third millennium BCE.
Like Qoheleth, that Egyptian recounts a conversation with himself (his
soul, his heart) about one's reputation and a preference for death.
Only excerpts can be quoted, but the tone, though more negative than
that of Qoheleth, sounds very familiar.

> Behold, my name is detested,
> Behold, more than the smell of vultures
> On a summer's day when the sky is hot
>
> Behold, my name is detested,
> Behold, (more than the smell of) a catch of fish
> On a day of catching when the sky is hot...

---

1. *Rā'ā* here probably connotes 'enjoyment' rather than simply 'sight', a
frequent meaning in biblical Hebrew.

To whom can I speak today?
I am heavy-laden with trouble
Through lack of an intimate friend.

To whom can I speak today?
The wrong which roams the earth,
There is no end to it.

Death is in my sight today
(As when) a sick man becomes well,
Like going out of doors after detention.

Death is in my sight today
Like the smell of myrrh,
Like sitting under an awning on a windy day.[1]

Much later, and closer to the time of Qoheleth we hear similar advice in the words of Ahikar.

My son, better is a friend that is near than a brother that is far away, and better is a *good name* than much beauty; because a good name standeth for ever, and beauty grows old and becomes corrupted.

My son, *better is death than life* to the man that hath no rest; and better is the sound of lamentation in the ears of a fool than singing and joy.[2]

There are worse circumstances than death, and Qoheleth identifies them. We have already noted that a stillborn is better off than those whom Qoheleth and Ahikar refer to as having 'no rest' (6.5). Elsewhere, other specific reasons for such a preference are given. He concludes about one type of entrapment, 'And I found more bitter than death the woman whose heart is snares and nets, and whose hands are fetters; he who pleases God escapes her, but the sinner is taken by her' (7.26). That she is more bitter than death may not necessarily be hyperbolic. The physical and emotional turmoil following this type of an affair could torment a sensitive soul and well drive one to the same conclusion. This is not necessarily then a hyperbolic statement, but a statement of fact.

In one of Qoheleth's most emotional vignettes we see his sensitivity to the victims of power, victims who might prefer death over life.

---

1. Faulkner, 'Tired of Life', pp. 27-29.
2. A.E. Goodman, 'The Words of Ahikar', in D.W. Thomas (ed.), *Documents from Old Testament Times* (New York: Harper & Row, 1961), p. 273.

> Again I saw all the oppressions that are practiced under the sun. And
> behold, the tears of the oppressed, and they had no one to comfort them!
> On the side of their oppressors there was power, and there was no one to
> comfort them.[1] And I thought the dead who are already dead more fortu-
> nate than the living who are still alive; but better than both is he who has
> not yet[2] been, and has not seen the evil deeds that are done under the sun
> (4.1-3).

If there only had been *some* relief, this solemn blessing on both the
dead and those not yet alive presumably would not have been as readily on the lips of Qoheleth. Though he laments often over this tragic
world fraught with burdens and tyrannical pressures, he would rather
call upon joy from every crevice of that rough terrain to buffer the
jolts along the way. But that there is *no one* nor *anything* to comfort
them, this is for Qoheleth worse than death. Rather than life then,
death is the consolation for those whose torment is inextinguishable.[3]

The transience of life is also expressed by Qoheleth in conjunction
with his phrases 'after me', 'after him', and in the context of human
ignorance of events following death. On the one hand this is a source
of great despair for him since the possibility of a fool taking control
of one's posthumous estate renders the value of one's lifelong efforts
tentative at best:

> I hated all my toil in which I had toiled under the sun, seeing that I must
> leave it to the man who will come after me; and who knows whether he
> will be a wise man or a fool? Yet he will be master of all for which I
> toiled and used my wisdom under the sun (2.18, 19).

> For who knows what is good for man while he lives the few days of his
> fleeting life, which he passes like a shadow? For who can tell man what
> will be after him under the sun? (6.12).

Yet the same unfathomableness of the future is also an incentive for
one to enjoy life *now*:

1. To emotion should be attributed this repeated phrase 'no one to comfort
them', not to a scribal error as has been suggested.
2. It is important that 'not *yet*' is the phrase here as opposed to 'never'. With
this unique adverb ('*ăden*) he implies the transience of the oppression, and an optimism of better days. Knowing that there is an appointed time for birth and death
(3.2), the delay of one's birth could end in escaping the treachery of a given day and
age.
3. However, he does not go as far as to condone suicide or ending another's life
on the basis of the estimation of one's potential quality of life.

> So I saw that there is nothing better than that a man should enjoy his
> work, for that is his lot; who can bring him to see what will come after
> him? (3.22).

Since curiosity about events subsequent to life must end at just that,
curiosity, such speculations can only distract one from any happiness
that is currently available. Qoheleth thereby convicts himself of folly
in his initial reaction of hatred and despair of life and labor recorded
in 2.18-23. Echoing the conclusions in 2.24-26, here in 3.22, the
explicit correction of that despair is found again. I will discuss this
further in Chapter 3.

There is a reason for the frustration of not knowing the future:
God's plan involves a design of life's experiences so that any conjec-
tures of this sort are totally in vain. So the only option left is to be
happy in those days of prosperity that occasionally come one's way:

> In the day of prosperity be joyful, and in the day of adversity consider;
> God has made the one as well as the other, so that man may not find out
> anything that will be after him (7.14 cf. 3.14).

Consequently, he cannot count on his own achievements being
extended indefinitely after death, hoping to extend the value of his life
by associating with those accomplishments that might outlive him.
Regardless of the longevity of those achievements, he has enough with
which to delight himself without wasting energies on such apprehensions. Life is too short to spend any proportion of it attempting to
measure the immeasurable. Yet such speculations are characteristic of
the fool and his conversations, and they end without fail in only
meaningless chatter: 'A fool multiplies words, though no man knows
what is to be, and who can tell him what will be after him?' (10.14 cf.
5.3, 7). Certainly such foolish prognistications neglect the real
pleasures at hand.

Actually there is something that can be known about all events on
the earth after one's inevitable death, namely that the same things that
have always occurred on earth will recur: 'what can the man do who
comes after the king? Only what he has already done' (2.12; cf. 1.9,
10). Though Qoheleth accentuates this cyclicity of all activities, he
cautions against squandering an already ephemeral life by trying to
imagine any more specifically what the future might hold.

Finally, any consolation to death that Qoheleth might have drawn from an afterlife is very typical of the other Hebrew biblical literature: undeveloped.[1] This is not the place to discuss at length the Hebrew view or views of resurrection, primarily because it factors little in any of Qoheleth's arguments. In fact, it is exactly the uncertainty of the nature of life after death that figures significantly in his argument about enjoying life now, as we saw above. But that his rhetorical question of 3.21 anticipates a later affirmative answer in 12.7 is quite clear.

> Who knows whether the breath (*rûaḥ*) of man goes upward and the breath of the beast goes down to the earth? (3.21).

> The dust returns to the earth as it was, and the breath (*rûaḥ*) returns to the God who gave it (12.7).[2]

The question remains what the nature of that afterlife was for Qoheleth. We do not know, and cannot know, but whatever it was it was not his decision to employ it as a substantial consolation.

Qoheleth's broad coverage of death proves he is fully aware of human finitude in abilities as well as life. He approaches his investigation with this realistic tenet—life is impermanent. But he also accentuates the balancing remissions available in the face of death's horrid image. It is more than possible to interpret and translate Qoheleth's *hevel* statements along the line of life's *brevity*, distinct from any notion of futility, vanity, emptiness or meaninglessness. Pleasure and wisdom are repeatedly commended in spite of death, and as prevalent as absurdities or ironies in life might be, they do not define the essence of life. Life is a gift of God and must be judged existentially whether it is a greater or lesser blessing. Tragedy is real, torment and oppression are frequent, but they are not *always* the substance of *everybody's* life. There is at least one universal condition—transience, and Qoheleth reminds us of it on a number of occasions.

---

1. Ogden (*Qoheleth, passim*) is one of those most open to a possible hope of Qoheleth in some 'advantage' after death. Contrast for example, A. Schoors, 'Koheleth: A Perspective of Life After Death?', *ETL* 61 (1985), pp. 295-303.

2. It is doubtful that all questions in Qoheleth beginning with 'Who knows', anticipate the negative answer, 'no one knows'. Though Crenshaw does show where this is the expected answer (2.19), the instances of it in 6.12 and 8.1 do not demand the negative: 'The Expression of *mî yôdēaʿ* in the Hebrew Bible', *VT* 36 (1986), pp. 274-88.

Chapter 3

EPHEMERAL EFFORTS

As for the duration of what is done on the earth,
It is a kind of dream.

An Egyptian Harper*

'Temporary, temporary', says the Speaker, 'temporary, temporary, total
transience. What advantage is there to a man in all his toil under the sun?'

If 'all is breath' or 'total transience' is a clear observation for
Qoheleth's investigation, then 'what advantage (*yitrôn*)'[1] is the governing question that guides his search. He asks it often as he searches
for wisdom, and his answer is quite consistent. First, the question asks
what advantage there is to one's 'labor' or 'toil', an expression denoting exertion rather than simple 'deeds' or 'activities'. The arduous tasks
of life are described effectively elsewhere, for example, 'all his days
are full of pain, and his work is a vexation; even in the night his mind
does not rest' (2.23). This question of advantage then is emotionally
laden, and erupts from the frustrated yet responsible laborer who is
looking for that advantage which would justify his exhaustive efforts.[2]

---

*   *ANET*, p. 34.
1.   The view that *yitrôn* has an implicit commercial denotation does not take into
account that Qoheleth's curiosity touches on every aspect of life, not simply the business dealings of the day. The meaning of the root, *yātar*, is much more inclusive,
pertaining to anything that has been left or which remains (BDB, p. 451). Thus
'advantage' and 'profit' are probably the most appropriate renditions, if the latter also
is left more room in which to operate than the business milieu alone. For an example
of how it may at times be commercial, see J.L. Kugel, 'Qoheleth and Money', *CBQ*
51 (1989), pp. 43-44.
2.   The noun and verb of '*āmāl* appear some 35 times in Ecclesiastes,
sometimes in the cognate phrasing with '*āsāh*, and both noun and verb forms appear
some 50 times. The significance of effort for Qoheleth is unquestionable.

In other words, given the transience of everything, is it really worth it?

The challenge of finding some 'advantage' then becomes the driving motivation to follow Qoheleth as he steps out to comb the terrain. This is his quest on which he embarks with a preliminary observation, 'I have seen everything that is done under the sun; and behold all is temporary and like the will of the wind' (1.14).

Qoheleth poses this exact question on five occasions, but only in the first half of his speech. The first occurs in 1.3, the next in 3.9:

> What advantage has the laborer from his labor?

and later, three times within the same literary unit, 5.10–6.9:

> What advantage[1] has the owner? (5.11)
>
> What advantage has he who toiled for the wind? (5.16)
>
> What advantage has the wise man over the fool? (6.8)

The same question is asked in slightly different terms, asking what is 'good' (*tôb*) for humanity in life (2.3, 6.8) and simply, what 'is' there for a man in all his labor (2.22). These equivalent forms of this governing question continue to penetrate the whole of Ecclesiastes and are especially helpful in truly hearing his answer, since it is also voiced in these exact terms.

Actually, his answer to what advantages, or what good, can come to a man in a life of turmoil and effort follows two lines. First, wisdom in life leads directly to several benefits. Qoheleth commends wisdom explicitly for its *yitrôn* in itself, and the *yitrôn* it can provide. The difference between wisdom and folly is the difference between day and night:

> Then I saw that there is an advantage (*yitrôn*) to wisdom over folly, as the advantage (*yitrôn*) of light over darkness (2.13).

Later he asserts,

> Wisdom is good with an inheritance,
>   and an advantage (*yōtēr*) to those who see the sun.

---

1. In this case the synonym *kišrôn* is used for *yitrôn* as it is in Eccl. 4.4; 10.10; 11.6. For the meaning of *kišrôn* in Ecclesiastes, see Fredericks, *Qoheleth's Language*, pp. 184-85, 199-200, 229.

> For the protection of wisdom is like the protection of money;
>   and the advantage (*yitrôn*) of knowledge is that wisdom preserves
>   the life of him who has it (7.11, 12).[1]

He is also realistic enough to conclude that profit is certainly gained by a competitive spirit:

> Then I saw that all toil and advantage in work come from a man's rivalry with his neighbor (4.4a).

But on the more positive side, he identifies the protective element of wisdom when cautioning against careless and improper professional technique (10.8-10); he concludes and illustrates that,

> The advantage (*yitrôn*) of wisdom gives success.[2] If the serpent bites before it is charmed, there is no advantage (*yitrôn*) to the charmer.

And a wise king is an advantage (*yitrôn*) to his land (5.9). He also recognizes the supporting role of wisdom in his very search *for* wisdom (2.9).

These explicit advantages of wisdom may not be all that Qoheleth seeks when enquiring whether an arduous life is worth it, but it is a significant part of the total answer. Additional advantages are expressed through what are 'good' or 'better' pursuits in life. Just as the *question* may be asked by *yitrôn* or *tôb*, the *answers* can be expressed in either way as well. 'What advantage is there in one's laborious life? What good is there?' Literally there is 'good' (*tôb*) in the larger profit gained by a partnership (4.9), in the wisdom even of the poor (4.13 cf. 9.15), in paying vows (5.4, 5), in an honorable reputation (7.1), in sober reflection on death (7.2, 4), in receiving rebuke favorably (7.5), in patience (7.8), in wisdom's strength (9.16) and in wisdom's success (9.18). Many other benefits of wisdom are mentioned by Qoheleth, but these expressed by *yitrôn* or *tôb* are the most obvious components of an answer to his questions which are asked with the same terms.

Actually Qoheleth answers his thematic question even more directly than this. After phrasing this question, he moves on immediately at

---

1. Challenges appear in the syntax of this phrase though the intention is still clear enough. For an argument for our preference here, see A. Frendo, 'The "Broken Construct Chain" in Qoh. 10.10b', *Bib* 62 (1981), pp. 544-45.

2. Two very helpful articles on this topic come from Ogden: 'The "Better"-Proverb (*tôb-spruch*), Rhetorical Criticism, and Qoheleth', *JBL* 96 (1977), pp. 489-505; 'Qoheleth's Use of the "Nothing is Better"-form', *JBL* 98 (1979), pp. 339-50.

times to answer with no uncertainty. The answer, like the question, is phrased in equally formulaic style, that is, the 'nothing better' form.[1]

> *What has a man* from all the toils and strain with which he toils under the sun? For all his days are full of pain, and his work is a vexation; even in the night his mind does not rest. This also is temporary. *There is nothing better for a man* than that he should eat and drink, and find enjoyment in his toil. This also, I saw, is from the hand of God; for apart from him who can eat or who can have enjoyment? (2.22-25).
>
> *What advantage* does the laborer have in his labor?...I know that *there is nothing better* for them than to rejoice and to do good in one's lifetime, moreover, that every man who eats and drinks and sees good in all his labor—it is the gift of God (3.9, 12, 13).

Elsewhere it is answered in slightly different words:

> *What advantage (kišrôn)* is there for the owner but for his eyes to enjoy [his property] (5.11).
>
> *What advantage (yitrôn)* has the wise man over the fool?...*Better* is the enjoyment of the eyes than the wandering of the soul (6.8, 9).

Clearly the advantage to the individual from toil is the enjoyment of the labor itself and its consequent fruits, however simple they might be. The theme of pleasure and enjoyment will be addressed fully in the next chapter, so I will only outline its relevance here, but the pervasiveness of this theme (also 3.22, 5.18-20, 8.15, 9.7-9, 11.7-10), and the extremely positive frame in which it is cast go a long way to show that to some degree Qoheleth's search is satisfied. Herein lies precisely the real tragedy of the solitary man of 4.8, who labors endlessly and yet does not have the key *advantage* to those labors—pleasure. If he does not enjoy the fruit, he personally has no one else to enjoy them for him. This is exactly what Qoheleth despairs of in his own case,

> So I turned and gave my heart up to despair over all the toil of my labors under the sun, because sometimes a man who has toiled with wisdom and knowledge and skill must leave all to be enjoyed by a man who did not toil for it (2.20, 21).

Now when Qoheleth revives his questions at the mid-point of his speech (6.11, 12), we see a reunion of these two equivalent phrases

---

1.   I prefer the moral slant on this phrase, 'do good', rather than the amoral 'fair well' (Greek *eŭ práttein*). This will come up again later in Chapter 5.

pertaining to advantage (*yitrôn* and *tôb*), along with the governing
presupposition of temporality.

> What *advantage* (*yōtēr*) is there to man? For who knows what is *good* for
> man while he lives the *few days* of his *brief life* which he passes like a
> *shadow*?

Qoheleth does not intend to remind us of any futility in our search so
far, since we have been presented clearly with the advantages of wisdom and enjoyment. Furthermore, both wisdom and enjoyment are
nothing less than gifts of God himself (2.26; also 2.24, 3.13; 5.19).
Instead these serve simultaneously as summary and introductory questions, designed to encourage the listeners to regroup their efforts and
watch for further answers in the remaining half of the speech. We
have the answers essentially already, but Qoheleth will continue to
confirm them now; and he does not waste much time, delving into the
advantages of wisdom in the very next verses of Chapter 7.

If there is such an overwhelming affirmative answer to the question
of whether there is an advantage, why then do we hear in 2.11 that
there was '*no* advantage'?

> And whatever my eyes desired I did not keep from them; I kept my heart
> from no pleasure, for my heart found pleasure in all my toil, and this was
> my reward for all my toil (2.10).

So far so good. One would expect a conclusion like this, given our
brief survey of what Qoheleth thinks about toil. But 2.11 is a puzzling
continuation.

> Then I considered all that my hands had done and the toil I had spent in
> doing it, and behold, all was temporary and like the will of the wind, so
> there was *no profit* under the sun.

Any resolution to an apparent contradiction in 2.10 and 2.11 is to be
found in what follows, in both the content and its emotional context.
As he looks at his own personal toil and accomplishments, Qoheleth is
forced to feel about himself what he so far had only generalized about
everyone else (1.12-14): achievements are of only a *transient* value.
They are valuable (2.10), but only for the moment. As he reacts to the
limited value of his labor, he prematurely blurts out that there is *no*
value. The exceptional nature of this general conclusion is shown not
only through its absence in the rest of the speech, and its explicit
contradiction everywhere else, but also in his very resolution to the
problem found in 2.22-26. Like his temperamental 'I hated life...

I hated all my toil...gave up my heart to despair...' (2.17, 18, 20), he over-reacts and concludes that there was 'no advantage' to his endeavors. But he follows this cathartic outburst with the clear conclusion only a few verses later in 2.24, 25:

> There is nothing better for a man than that he should eat and drink, and find enjoyment in his toil. This also, I saw, is from the hand of God; for apart from him who can eat or who can have enjoyment?

This then is part of a temporary 'disillusionment'[1] that is not characteristic of Qoheleth in the rest of his observations and conclusions. He generalizes about such mellowing in the wise person in a proverbial fashion later in 8.1: 'A man's wisdom makes his face shine, and the hardness of his countenance is changed'. This is a fact even in this very speech.

On one other occasion he reports '*no* advantage'—specifically in respect to the equally inevitable death for beast and man, he reasonably concludes there is no advantage for humanity (3.19-21). The context narrows the scope of 'no advantage' to the *longevity* of life, not the *value* of life. Though there is no advantage in respect to death, Qoheleth wants to assure us that there is still an advantage for man in life, since his next statement, in the 'nothing better' form, tells us what we have heard and will hear again,

> So I saw that there is nothing better than that a man should enjoy his work, for that is his lot (3.22).

His most dramatic momentary despair in ch. 2 is caused primarily by the transitory value of all his efforts. An obvious and critical reason for this limited value is that the laborer himself is a passing event. The transience of the individual gives only a tentative status to his successful, even wise, efforts. His early outburst to this effect is found in that cathartic phase in 2.14-16b, but later he returns to the subject much more subdued.

---

1. Whybray, 'Joy', p. 92. Regardless of one's view of Ecclesiastes as an optimistic or pessimistic book some degree of qualification is necessary when describing Qoheleth's conclusions about 'advantage'. For example, from one who sees Qoheleth's view of the value of life to be more pessimistic ('Es ist eben alles Scheisse' ['Die unveränderbare Welt', in W. Schotroff and W. Stegemann (eds.), *Der Gott der Kleinen Leute* (Munich: Kaiser, 1979), p. 57]), Crüsemann admits 'Koheleth is able to assign wisdom a relative "gain" (as in 2.13; 7.12; 10.10). He is certainly not unjustified to do so, we may say; he lives by it' ('The Unchangeable World', p. 66).

His outbursts in ch. 2 eventually mellow into advice in ch. 9: not only should one enjoy his fleeting labors, but one had better make them count.

> For the living know that they will die, but the dead know nothing, and they have no more reward, for their memory is forgotten. The dead's love, and their hate, and their envy have *already perished*, and they have *no more for ever* any share in all that is done under the sun... Whatever your hand finds to do, do it with your might; for there is no work or thought or knowledge or wisdom in Sheol, to which you are going (9.6, 10; cf. 5.15).

The sentiments of the *Gilgamesh Epic* are similar.[1]

> Do we build a house for ever?
> Do we seal (contracts) for ever?
> Do brothers divide shares for ever?
> Does hatred persist for ever in [the land]?...
> Since the days of yore there has been no [permanence];
> The resting and the dead, how alike [they are]!
> Do they not compose a picture of death,
> The commoner and the noble,
> Once they are near to [their fate]?

In 9.5 quoted above, we see another reason why the value of the deceased's labors are so restricted: 'they have no more reward, for their memory is forgotten'. Any reward one might hope for in being remembered by all generations is a pipe dream. Qoheleth wrestles with this, considering it to be no incidental annoyance, but a travesty worth highlighting frequently. He is aware of it in general principle,

> There is no remembrance of former things, nor will there be any remembrance of later things yet to happen among those who come after (1.11).

But he also experiences this personally and it becomes part of that awful realization that unsettled him in ch. 2. He sees no future in his accomplishments being recollected (2.15, 16). However, what

---

1. *ANET*, pp. 92-93. It is a similar passage in the *Gilgamesh Epic* that Loretz sees as the source of Qoheleth's conviction that all is *hevel*: 'As for Mankind numbered are their days; whatever they achieve is but the wind (*šāru*)!' (*ANET*, p. 79). Though the conjunction of life and efforts is a striking parallel to Ecclesiastes, and though *wind* and *hevel* do have related semantic fields, M. Dahood's objection is forceful: since Qoheleth had *rûaḥ* at his disposal, which is a closer parallel to *šāru* (wind) than *hevel*, a strong and direct influence is improbable (Dahood's review of Loretz' *Qohelet*, *Bib* 46 [1964], pp. 234-36).

disappointed him in his earlier concerted research into matters of folly and wisdom, eventually becomes a developed idea in his parable of the besieged city:

> There was a little city with few men in it; and a great king came against it, building great siegeworks against it. But there was found in it a poor wise man, and he by his wisdom delivered the city. Yet no one remembered that poor man (9.14, 15).

For Qoheleth, it is a matter of justice that honorable and wise achievements be remembered, but in his characteristic realism he knows better, and goes on to deduce from it other adages in 9.16–10.1. The temporary value to labor, then, is based in one's own ephemerality, but it is confirmed by everyone else's fleeting memory.

Furthermore, achievements are not only forgotten, but even those achievements that may survive one's death are themselves in danger of being shattered by successors:

> I hated all my toil in which I had toiled under the sun, seeing that I must leave it to the man who will come after me; and who knows whether he will be a wise man or a fool? (2.18, 19a; cf. Ps. 39.6).

The implication is that a wise successor would respect Qoheleth's efforts and perpetuate them. But a fool would inevitably mishandle the affairs, and the achievements would end. The fruit of one's labor left precariously in the hands of another person are often disgraced by mutilation if not annihilation. Both death, and the disrespect of others shown by both their neglectful memories and foolish destruction, are seen by Qoheleth to be disheartening terminations of even the most glorious efforts.

Yet another reason that there is no lasting profit to one's efforts is that there is nothing innovative nor especially unique about them. One's labor never includes something adequately singular in its achievement that it will enjoy endless distinction and stand above the efforts of everyone else. Whatever it is, it has been done before:

> What has been is what will be, and what has been done is what will be done; and there is nothing new under the sun. Is there a thing of which it is said, 'It is new'? It has been already in the ages before us (1.9, 10; cf. 2.12, 6.10).

This is not due to the lack of human ingenuity alone, but is somehow an objective of God (as is everything for Qoheleth): 'That which is, already has been; that which is to be, already has been; for God seeks what has passed'.[1] God's sovereign design, therefore, is to assure the cyclicity of human events, just as it is to assure cyclicity of the rest of the created order (1.3-11). The interplay of Qoheleth's thematic question (1.3), and the following poem on cyclicity is an indirect question-answer sequence. The following poem emphasizes the circular motions of nature, including humanity. And if all truly is circular, then what better metaphors to use than 'breath', the lifelong alternation of inhalations and exhalations, and the 'will of the wind', which follows its circular courses (1.6)? A breath is as rhythmic as it is brief; though a desire of the wind is impermanent and ever-changing, it is bound to return; though one's activities are temporary, they are sure to be reiterated. What then is the advantage in one's efforts? Whatever the advantage, it will be neither in their duration nor uniqueness. Human endeavors are only temporary, to be repeated by those who follow but re-enacted with neither reference nor credit given to the original renditions of those activities.

The temporality of efforts is made a theme of Qoheleth's 'poem of seasons', (3.1-8) quoted already in Chapter 1. All events in this poem are volitional (except for the first two: birth and death), and it is clear that these actions or reactions in life are for limited times only. They are cyclical by and large, some performed frequently, others hopefully less often. Of course the poem lends itself to many interpretations of its purpose in Ecclesiastes; some see it as only further proof of human futility since God has predestined all anyway.[2] However, God's sovereignty is not an impediment to advising wisdom even in the 'classical' age, where God's sovereign determinism is set alongside human responsibility.

> Commit your work to the Lord,
>> and your plans will be established.
> The Lord has made everything for its purpose, even the wicked for the
>> day of trouble (Prov. 16.3, 4).
>
> No wisdom, no understanding, no counsel,
>> can avail against the Lord.

---

1. See the commentaries on what it is exactly that God is seeking, in addition to R.B. Salters, 'A Note on the Exegesis of Ecclesiastes 3.15b', *ZAW* 88 (1976), pp. 419-22.
2. E.g. Gordis, *Koheleth*, pp. 228-29.

The horse is made ready for the day of battle,
      but the victory belongs to the Lord (Prov. 21.30, 31 cf. 19.21).

Others see the poem emphasizing the unknowability of the proper time for all our activities.[1] Though Qoheleth does admit severe limitations in human knowledge, he does so primarily in respect to knowledge of the future (e.g. 8.7). But for the present, he is not reticent to advise appropriate action at the appropriate time, for example:

He who obeys a command will meet no harm and a wise man's heart
knows a time and procedure, for every matter has its time and procedure,
although man's trouble lies heavy upon him (8.5, 6).

He instructs that there is a seasonal advisability to every action. Each act has its own temporary suitability. Though these apt efforts may be only transitory, they are nonetheless commendatory, and Qoheleth often speaks as the traditional sage who sees the highest priority in ordering one's life. In fact, it is the very transience of an endeavor's suitability that helps define its wisdom. To know the correct timing of affairs is for Qoheleth the zenith of wisdom. Though that knowledge certainly is not exhaustive, it is to the honor of the wise to calculate that timing correctly, and to do so often.

Rhetorically, the poem is intended to be a consolation for the fact of death which so distressed Qoheleth in ch. 2 and was reverted to in 3.18-22. Birth and death are according to God's timing (3.2a), wisdom must be applied within the daily responsibilities of the individual (3.2b-8). The poem then does not describe life's futility, but advises prudence and initiative not only to recognize the time, but also to respond with the most apt behavior. It does not demand resignation nor despair, rather it emphasizes how the momentary timeliness of wise activities is a microcosm of the eternal plan and wisdom of God. God is wise, we are to be wise. He does everything beautifully in its time, we are to strive to do the same. His actions are eternal, though ours are only seasonal. The meteoric nature of human effort is in clear contrast to the eternality of God's acts (3.14; cf. 7.13). This is why the earth stands 'forever' (1.4), it is *God's* creation, created for a

1. E.g. Crenshaw, *Ecclesiastes*, p. 92. Though 7.23, 24 speak of the inaccessability of wisdom, the two verses must be qualified by the assertion that Qoheleth did discover some wisdom, evidenced in the very next verses. Qoheleth is given to hyperbole at times, but not in a confusing or even contradicting fashion; only exaggerating initially with clear mitigating statements to follow.

constant backdrop to the repeat performances of generation after generation. These performances can be absurdly comical, made up of scenes and acts of utter folly and futility, or they, though brief, can be brilliant re-enactments of conventional wisdom.

Foolish performances are epitomized in Ecclesiastes by the babbling fool. This is not surprising since in the book of Proverbs the plurality of proverbs deal with wise and foolish speech.[1] Qoheleth's fundamental principle could be summarized by 3.7b: 'A time to keep silence, and a time to speak' (cf. 9.17). But the fool is either not aware, or intentionally ignores the fact that like everything else, speaking has its most effective timeliness.

> To make an apt answer is a joy to a man,
> and a word in season, how good it is! (Prov. 15.23).

> Even a fool who keeps silent is considered wise;
> when he closes his lips, he is deemed intelligent (Prov. 17.28).

The problems of speaking hastily and excessively to God and man are therefore emphasized by Qoheleth. Lack of restraint in one's promises to God, both in when they are given, and what they entail, is a serious mistake (5.1-7). Promises that have merely dreams and garrulity as their substance cannot be sustained or kept, and eventually end in the sin of broken vows. Qoheleth therefore concurs with conventional wisdom:

> It is better that you should not vow, than you should vow and not pay
> (Eccl. 5.5).

> It is a snare for a man to say rashly,
> 'It is holy',
> and to reflect only after making his vows (Prov. 20.25).

But apart from vows, chatter of any sort is instantaneously ineffective, and is only more foolish as the statements lengthen (6.11, 10.12-15 cf. 5.3).

---

1.   E.g. 10.10, 11, 13, 18, 19, 20, 21, 31, 32; 11.9, 11, 12, 13; 12.6, 13, 14, 17, 18, 19, 20, 22, 23, 25; 13.2, 3, 5, 14; 14.3, 5, 7, 25; 15.1, 2, 4, 7, 23, 28; 16.21, 23, 24, 27, 28, 30; 17.14, 19, 20, 27, 28; 18.2, 4, 6, 7, 8, 13, 20, 21; 19.5, 9; 20.3, 15, 25; 21.23, 28; 22.11; 23.9; 24.26; 25.8, 9, 10, 11, 14, 15, 18, 20, 23; 26.4, 5, 7, 18, 19, 20, 21, 22, 23, 24, 25, 26, 28; 27.14; 28.13; 29.5, 20; 30.5, 6, 10, 32, 33.

Folly in speech can also come by cursing and complaining. Cursing the king could be serious (10.20). On the other hand, being cursed oneself by a servant should be ignored (7.21). After all, no one is righteous continually, including the person who is victimized by gossips (7.20, 21). Furthermore, complaints about how the good-old-days have passed, and that nothing is the same anymore, are also foolishness: 'Say not, "Why were the former days better than these?" for it is not from wisdom that you ask this' (7.10). Complaints like these are futile, and true wisdom will ignore them since God is the master of time and events, and complaining about his designs is simply chirp and chatter:

> Consider the work of God; who can make straight what he has made crooked? In the day of prosperity be joyful, and in the day of adversity consider; God has made the one as well as the other, so that man may not find out anything that will be after him (7.13, 14).

Next to tiresome speech is the equally transient experience of frivolity. Qoheleth draws a significant line when recommending pleasures but denigrating hilarity. Mirthful pleasure is part of Qoheleth's search for wisdom, but quite expectedly it is fleeting too (*hevel*) (2.1, 2). Worse yet, a preoccupation with frivolity is superficial in addition to being but breath (7.2-6): 'For as the crackling of thorns under a pot, so is the laughter of the fools. This also is temporary' (7.6). Making matters even worse, gluttony, drunkenness and greed are frequent companions of insidious mirth (10.16, 17, 19).

Qoheleth is convinced that much effort is motivated by envy, and, like all efforts, ends in what is merely transitory. He conveys such temporary value by two different yet characteristic expressions.

> Then I saw that all toil and all advantage in work come from a man's envy of his neighbor. This also is *temporary* (*hevel*) and like the *will of the wind* (4.4).

> Their love their hate and their envy have *already* (*kĕbār*) perished, and they have no more for ever a share in all that is done under the sun (9.6).

This competitiveness, however, is inferior to the potential advantages in cooperation. Following his comments on rivalry (4.4) and solitary toil (4.7, 8), Qoheleth highly recommends the extra profit that can come from amiable partnerships (4.7-12). 'What advantage is there in one's toil?' With another person there is a better profit, including covering for each other's weaknesses, generating warmth and victory over an adversary.

Qoheleth further advises moderation in one's toils by two consecutive proverbs, which approach the issue from opposite ends of the question.

The fool folds his hands, and eats his flesh (4.5).

Better is a handful of rest than two hands' full of toil and the will of the wind (4.6).

Stated negatively, sloth is self-destructive. Positively stated, some rest is better than restless toil which will end in only a temporary reward anyway. His advice reminds one of Prov. 23.4, 5.

Do not toil to acquire wealth;
    be wise enough to desist.
When your eyes light upon it, it is gone;
    for suddenly it takes to itself wings,
    flying like an eagle toward heaven.

Then follows the illustration of 4.7, 8 of the solitary man who has no pleasure. This advice is certainly typical for the conventional sage,[1] and Qoheleth is also convinced of its truth since on three other occasions he recommends diligence with his characteristic frankness.

Through sloth the roof sinks in,
    and through indolence the house leaks (10.18).

He who observes the wind will not sow;
    and he who regards the clouds will not reap...
In the morning sow your seed, and at evening withhold not your hand
    (11.4, 6a).

Whatever your hand finds to do, do it with your might; for there is no work or thought or knowledge or wisdom in Sheol, to which you are going (9.10).

In a couple of verses that seem completely out of any context, Qoheleth praises a responsible, vigilant king (5.8, 9). Between the cohesive 5.1-7 and symmetrical 5.10–6.9, we find this counsel:

---

1.   The importance of diligence in classical wisdom is obvious, e.g. 10.4, 5, 26; 12.11, 24, 27; 13.4; 14.23; 15.19; 16.26; 18.9; 19.15, 24; 20.4, 13; 21.5, 25, 26; 22.13, 29; 24.10, 27, 30-34; 26.13, 14, 15, 16; 27.18, 23-27; 28.19; 30.15.

If you see the poor oppressed and justice and righteousness violated, do not be amazed at the matter; for the high official is watched by a higher one, and there are yet higher ones over them. Generally, an advantage of a land is a king devoted to a cultivated field (5.8, 9).[1]

One should not be surprised nor alarmed at injustice, and generally should find some relief in the fact that a king can profit his country by keeping his bureaucracy in order. By tending his governmental personnel, removing the weeds, softening the soil, the administration of the land should be more just and less intimidating to the people. The agri-king figure appears in Proverbs as well, and is one who insures righteousness.

A wise king winnows the wicked,
    and drives the threshing-wheel over them.
A king who sits on the throne of judgment
    winnows all evil with his eyes (Prov. 20.26, 8 cf. 14.35; 16.12; 28.2, 3; 29.12).

Many other categories of disciplined living are prescribed by Qoheleth. Admittedly they are qualified by his realistic realization that wisdom can be easily and disproportionately cancelled by only a little foolishness, thus making wisdom's effect on life all too brief (9.18; 10.1). Still, they too are representative of the confident, positive wisdom of Proverbs. Simply put, wisdom literature emphasizes the success of the individual, whereas the bulk of the remaining canonical literature ultimately concerns itself with the success of the nation. Personal success and its absence is *the* issue in Proverbs, Job and the wisdom psalms, and it is this specific guidance for individual success (advantage) in Ecclesiastes which mirrors that of these other wisdom texts. This is quite evident from additional parallels. Any view that Qoheleth quotes conventional wisdom to refine, qualify or reject it, needs to be qualified itself given the numerous quotes of complete agreement in other places where such a revisionist purpose for quoting is nowhere to be seen.

Teachableness

Better is a poor and wise youth, than an old and foolish king, who will no longer take advice (Eccl. 4.13).

---

1.   Any translation of this latter verse can only be tentative at best given its cryptic and seemingly impossible syntax. See the commentaries for other options.

It is better for a man to hear the rebuke of the wise than to hear the song
of fools (Eccl. 7.5).

The words of the wise heard in quiet are better than the shouting of a ruler
among fools (Eccl. 9.17).

He whose ear heeds wholesome admonition will abide among the wise
(Prov. 15.31).

Like a gold ring or an ornament of gold
is a wise reprover to a listening ear (Prov. 25.12).[1]

Bribery

Surely oppression makes the wise man foolish,
and a bribe corrupts the mind (Eccl. 7.7).

A wicked man accepts a bribe from the bosom
to pervert the ways of justice (Prov. 17.23).[2]

Personal Anger

Be not quick to anger,
for anger lodges in the bosom of fools (Eccl. 7.9).

A fool gives full vent to his anger,
but a wise man quietly holds it back (Prov. 29.11).

Another's Anger

If the anger of the ruler rises against you, do not leave your place, for
composure will make amends for great offenses (Eccl. 10.4).

A soft answer turns away wrath,
but a harsh word stirs up anger (Prov. 15.1).[3]

Insults

Do not give heed to all the things that men say, lest you hear your servant
cursing you; your heart knows that many times you have yourself cursed
others (Eccl. 7.21, 22).

1. Other proverbs on teachableness: 10.8, 17; 12.1, 15; 13.10, 13, 18; 15.12, 22,
32; 16.20; 17.10; 19.20, 25, 27; 20.18; 21.11; 24.5; 27.6, 9, 17; 28.9; 29.1.
2. Also Prov. 15.27; 17.8; 21.14; 29.4.
3. Also Prov. 10.12; 14.16, 17, 29; 16.32; 19.19; 25.28; 26.2; 27.3, 4; 29.8, 22;
30.32, 33.

The vexation of a fool is known at once,
　　but the prudent man ignores an insult (Prov. 12.16).

Compare also: *Professional technique*: Eccl. 10.8-10; 11.1, 2; Prov. 14.4, 27.23; *Excesses*: Eccl. 10.16, 17; Prov. 23.19-22;[1] *Strength in Wisdom*: Eccl. 7.19; 9.16, 18; 10.15, 17; Prov. 21.22; 24.5, 6; *Relationships with Women*: Eccl. 7.26; 9.9; Prov. 18.22, 22.14;[2] *Sovereignty of a King*: Eccl. 8.2-4, 10.4; Prov. 20.2.[3]

'What advantage is there for a man in his toil?' For Qoheleth the answer is not 'there is none', the answer assumed by many who see his thematic *hevel* to mean 'vanity, empty, absurd'. On the contrary, he says explicitly that there are many advantages to wisdom when one is able to discover it, and that pleasure and enjoyment are good and commendable pursuits to counterbalance one's exhaustive efforts. And the greater the wisdom, the more possible the pleasure. Pleasure, however, is also temporary, since the tragedies in this world will at times even torment the wise (1.17). But Qoheleth does not expect to enjoy life endlessly, any more than he expects to despair of life endlessly:

There is a time to weep, but a time to laugh
a time to mourn, but a time to dance.

1. Also Prov. 20.1; 21.17; 23.1-8, 19-22, 29-35; 25.16, 17; 27.20.
2. Also Prov. 12.4; 19.14; 23.26-28; 30.20.
3. Also Prov. 14.35; 16.13-15; 19.12; 20.2; 22.11; 25.6, 7.

Chapter 4

PASSING PLEASURES

Make holiday, and weary not therein!
Behold, it is not given to a man to take his property with him.
Behold, there is not one who departs who comes back again
                                        An Egyptian Harper*

Qoheleth's wholehearted recommendation of pleasure has already been identified as a critical theme of Ecclesiastes—one of the primary advantages to one's labor. In the previous chapter, the sources of that pleasure were described in only the most general way, but now it can be addressed more thoroughly. As positive as Qoheleth might be about enjoying life, as with everything else, it is only fleeting. Even though there are superficial and profound dimensions to pleasure in his estimation, their common feature is transience.[1] Nonetheless, as the primary consolation to the brevity of life and its efforts, pleasure, though transient does not render life vain.[2]

For him a distinction must be made between shallow frivolity and the substantially different rewards of pleasure that come ultimately from the very hand of God. Though there is a time to laugh (3.4),

---

* *ANET*, p. 467.

1. E.g. Gordis, *Koheleth*, p. 125: 'As for physical pleasure, it may offer a temporary satisfaction, but it is not an absolute or enduring good'. Those who have seen the significance of the theme of joy include Whybray, 'Joy'; Ogden, *Qoheleth*; Witzenrath, *Süss ist das Licht: Eine literaturewissenschaftliche Untersuchung zu Koh 11.7–12.7* (St Ottilien: EOS, 1979); R.K. Johnston, 'Confessions of an Workaholic: A Reappraisal of Qoheleth', *CBQ* 38 (1976), pp. 14-28; M.A. Klopfenstein, 'Die Skepsis des Kohelet', *TZ* 28 (1972), pp. 97-109.

2. In three separate passages, all three major ideas are found in close proximity: transience, advantage and enjoyment—2.22-26, 3.19-22, 6.8, 9.

laughter in itself can be that hollow noise that shatters the reverent solemnity of the contemplative spirit.

> I said of laughter 'It is mad' (2.2).

> For as the crackling of thorns under a pot,
>   so is the laughter of the fools;
> this also is transitory (7.6).

What better way to describe the obnoxious and ineffective value of frivolous laughter than to compare it to the equally brief and useless kindle of burning, crackling bramble? Such laughter is often untimely and always superficial, its value snaps away in an instant, and its sources are precisely the company and atmosphere to be avoided at all costs, even if the only option means frequenting the local morgue:

> The heart of the wise is in the house of mourning;
>   but the heart of fools is in the house of mirth (7.4).

Just such a house where levity and squandering indulgence prevails is re-examined later when the noble court is contrasted with the ignoble.

> Woe to you, O land, when your king is a child, and your princes feast in the morning! Happy are you, O land, when your king is the son of a free man, and your princes feast at the proper time, for strength and not for drunkenness! (10.16, 17).

These are not the type of pleasures that Qoheleth can bring himself to commend, rather they are objects of disdain set at a distance from the purest yet simplest pleasures of life.

Honorable opportunities for joy are regularly presented as mitigating gifts of which one should take advantage. A refrain is sung throughout Ecclesiastes, extolling the privileges of pleasurable experiences, and Whybray makes the astute observation that they 'are arranged in such a way as to state their theme with steadily increasing emphasis and solemnity'.[1]

> There is nothing better for a man than that he should eat and drink, and find enjoyment in his toil. This also, I saw, is from the *hand of God*: for apart from him who can eat or who can have enjoyment? (2.24, 25).[2]

1. Whybray, 'Joy', p. 87. His article on this particular subject is essential reading.
2. Many alternative meanings to *hûš*, which we render as 'enjoyment', have been offered. More than this single word makes the verse difficult to interpret, as any commentary will attest; but we follow the arguments of Levy, *Qohelet*, p. 78;

> I know that there is nothing better for them than to be happy and do good
> as long as they live; also that it is *God's gift* to man that everyone should
> eat and drink and take pleasure in all his labor...So I saw that there is
> nothing better than that a man should enjoy his work, for that is his
> lot...(3.12, 13, 22).

> Behold, what I have seen to be good and to be fitting is to eat and drink
> and find enjoyment in all the toil with which one toils under the sun the
> few days of his life which *God has given* him, for this is his lot (5.18).

> And I commend enjoyment, for man has no good thing under the sun but
> to eat, and drink, and enjoy himself, for this will go with him in his toil
> through the days of life which *God gives* him under the sun (8.15).

> Go, eat your bread with enjoyment, and drink your wine with a merry
> heart; for *God has already approved* what you do (9.7).

The commendation of such enjoyment is accentuated by the fact that
the source of such happiness is none other than God himself, who is
also the source of wisdom and further blessing (2.26).[1]

Qoheleth believes it is sweet simply to be alive, to be able to see the
sun (11.7). This is spoken of in the most general terms (2.25, 3.12,
4.8, 12.1), yet more specific means to happiness are recommended by
him as well. The fruits of one's toil are to be enjoyed around the table,
either directly, if a farmer, or indirectly through the marketplace.
These basic pleasures of food and drink are not to be despised as
minimal, insignificant blessings, but to be substantive sources of satisfaction in how they are prepared, and in the peace with which they are
consumed. This positive value of enjoying the fruit of one's labor,
found in verses like 9.7 above, is our encouragement to interpret 10.19
in a similar way.

> A feast is made for laughter and wine gladdens life and money pays for
> both.[2]

Lauha, *Kohelet*, p. 58; H.L. Ginsberg, *The Legend of King Keret* (New Haven:
American Schools of Oriental Research, 1946), p. 26; F. Rosenthal, review of
Ginsberg's *The Legend of King Keret*, *Or* 19 (1947), p. 402; M. Dahood, 'Qoheleth
and Recent Discoveries', *Bib* 39 (1958), pp. 307-308.

1.   'Through joy, God allows human beings to forget everything—themselves,
their death, the brevity of their lives' (Lohfink, 'The Present and Eternity', p. 240).
That God is also the source of tragedy, I will discuss in the next chapter.

2.   It would be nearly as easy to translate and interpret the words in the more
cynical sense that would follow from 10.18 about sloth. Yet since each of these
sources is spoken of as a blessing in Ecclesiastes, including money, it would *seem*

And money does more than purchase food and drink, it insures a degree of protection and security, necessary elements in a life where happiness is to abound (7.11, 12).

Now it is not only the fruit of toil that one is expected to enjoy in life, but according to most of the passages quoted above, the labor itself is to be enjoyed. Qoheleth advises in 3.22, 'So I saw that there is nothing better than that a man should enjoy his work'. Since to enjoy only the fruit would be disproportionate to the potentially gruelling and extended periods of labor needed to produce it, one should find and pursue that occupation which satisfies the vision and talents of the worker. Doing well in Ecclesiastes is primarily accomplished by acting wisely, something itemized generously by Qoheleth, and which is surely the origin of much of the happiness available in life. It is helpful to see that the identical Hebrew phrasing occurs in the 'what advantage' question and the positive answers provided by Qoheleth. The question as to the advantage *in* one's *toil* (*bĕ'āmāl*, or *bĕkol 'āmāl*; 1.3; 2.22) is answered repeatedly by what is *in* that toil to satisfy the worker (2.24; 3.13; 3.22, in his 'works'; 5.18; 8.15). There is then something in one's toils that provides an advantage, found both in the pleasures that ensue as well as those that reside *in* wise labor.

On the other hand, part of that wisdom will see the virtue in sensible rest.

> Better is a handful of quietness
> > than two hands full of toil and the will of the
> > wind (4.6)

Equally pleasant is a hard rest after hard work,

> Sweet is the sleep of the laborer,
> > whether he eats little or much;
> > but the satiety of the rich
> will not let him sleep (5.12).

In fact, rest can be so good that if the circumstances of life are unbearable, one's *final* rest is preferable to life itself (6.5).

Further pleasures are to be sought in experiencing a quality of life exemplified by clean, refreshing, presentable attire and appearance (9.8). White, the color of joy which contrasts with the black of

most probable that it carries the same message here; especially when feasting in itself is acceptable at the proper time in the noble court of the wise mentioned only two verses sooner. Our translation is influenced by Crenshaw, *Ecclesiastes*, p. 169.

mourning, is to be the characteristic scheme of the wardrobe of the wise, since unfortunately, there will be ample opportunity to wear the color of darkness, the blackness to which the deceased have descended. The blessings of spousal companionship are also recommended by Qoheleth who sees potential fulfilment through the love of another.

> Enjoy life with a woman whom you love, all the days of your brief life which he has given you under the sun, because that is your portion in life and in your toil (*ba'ămālkā*) which you labor under the sun (9.9).

The phrase '*a* woman whom you love' probably implies that one should choose such a woman to marry.[1] Be sure that she is one that he already loves, not a woman whom circumstances or other pressures seem to demand. Presumably, Qoheleth is addressing the young in this speech, some of whom could use the advice *before* the fact. The beauty of love between a man and a woman, rather than the wretched exploitation of adultery and prostitution is a common theme in Proverbs[2] and in the biblical literature in general. Qoheleth counsels as well that by all means one is to avoid the lure of the adulteress (7.26), and pursue the tranquility of life with an enjoyable, responsible woman.

In addition to the delights above, timely laughter, dancing and embracing, and love and peace are also pleasures encouraged by Qoheleth (3.4, 5, 8), resounding the advice of both the Babylonian *Gilgamesh Epic*, and an Egyptian counsel from a Harper:

> Though, Gilgamesh, let full be thy belly,
> Make thou merry by day and by night.

---

1.   The absence of the article has been seen to be yet another case of Qoheleth's irregular use of it—he really *did* want to specify *the* woman. For Qoheleth's overall use of the article according to biblical precedent, see Fredericks, *Qoheleth's Language*, pp. 15-17.

2.   E.g. Prov. 22.14; 23.26-28; 30.20. Needless to say, the wisdom of one's wife is also of value in wisdom literature. To reduce this allusion in Ecclesiastes to a purely sexual paradigm, e.g. Crüsemann ('The Unchangeable World', p. 69), would not reflect a true sage's estimation of the value of women (Prov. 31.10ff.; 12.4; 18.22; 19.14). Eccl. 7.28 in our estimation refers to the adulterous woman and those like her, found in the immediately preceding context (7.26), not to every woman everywhere. However, legitimate controversy has continued about Qoheleth's view of women. See for example Lohfink's 'War Kohelet ein Frauenfiend?', in *La sagesse de l'Ancien Testament* (Gembloux: Leuven University Press, 1979), pp. 257-87.

Of each day make though a feast of rejoicing,
Day and night dance thou and play!
Let thy garments be sparkling fresh,
Thy head be washed; bathe thou in water.
Pay heed to the little one that holds onto thy hand,
Let thy spouse delight in thy bosom![1]

Follow thy desire, as long as thou shalt live.
Put myrrh upon thy head and clothing of fine linen upon thee,
Being anointed with genuine marvels of the god's property.[2]

But Qoheleth's realism always curbs idealistic expectations. Again, the limited and only seasonable suitability of the diverse matters of daily existence itemized in 3.1-8 emphasizes the transience of even these pleasures. They will as a matter of course be replaced by seasons of weeping, mourning, separation, hatred and war (3.4, 5, 8). Yet not only the closure of seasons, but of life itself motivates Qoheleth's encouragements toward pleasure. Herein lies the same motivation as for the neighboring sages quoted above, who couch their calls to enjoyment within their laments over death as well.

Pleasure and benefits are addressed throughout Ecclesiastes, but . there are three extended passages that deal with the interplay of pleasure and its brevity. They are positioned symmetrically near the beginning (2.2-10), middle (5.10-6.9) and end (11.7-12.8) of Qoheleth's presentation. Furthermore, it appears that on this specific topic, he is especially creative, since each pericope has an involved rhetorical structure that I will attempt to highlight.

Qoheleth closes his speech by accentuating joy. But he does so in an urgent tone, since the impending debilitations of the aged and the cumulative disappointments through life's years take their toll on the vulnerable soul. A cache of memorable pleasures can at times be the only consolation.[3]

1. *ANET*, p. 90.
2. *ANET*, p. 467.
3. Without entering into the complicated disputes on the interpretation of 12.1-7, we take it to describe the effect of a powerful storm on a community (guards, nobleman, women grinders, etc.) and both its natural environment (trees, birds, etc.) and domestic equipment (bowls, rope, etc.). This storm is compared to the effect of dying and death on the individual and surrounding survivors. See Fredericks, 'Life's Storms and Structural Unity in Qoheleth 11.1–12.8', *JSOT* 52 (1991), pp. 95-114. For other articles on this section, see J.F.A. Sawyer, 'The Ruined House in Ecclesiastes 12: A Reconstruction of the Original Parable', *JBL* 94

> Light is sweet, and it is pleasant for the eyes to behold the sun. For if a
> man lives many years, let him rejoice in them all; but let him remember
> that the days of darkness will be many. All that comes is temporary.
> Rejoice, young man, in your youth, and let your heart cheer you in the
> days of your youth; walk in the ways of your heart and the sight of your
> eyes. But know that for all these things God will bring you into judgment.
> Remove vexation from your mind, and put away pain from your body;
> for youth and the dawn of life are fleeting. Remember also your Creator
> in the days of your youth, before the evil days come, and the years draw
> nigh, when you will say, 'I have no pleasure in them'; before the sun, the
> light, the moon, and the stars are darkened and clouds return after the
> rain...(11.7–12.2).

In this passage, death is at first only the backdrop for this urgency of
enjoyment, yet it moves gradually to the front of the stage and
becomes the main subject as 11.7–12.7 develops. His plea along the
way for reverence for both the Creator himself and his judgment,
quite expectedly qualifies Qoheleth's energetic charge to follow one's
desires wherever they lead.[1]

Ogden, building on H. Witzenrath's exposition, graphs this pro-
gression, showing how 11.8 itself outlines the rest of the pericope.[2]

11.8	If a man lives many years	Time Phrase
	let him *rejoice*	Theme A
	and *remember*	Theme B
	the days of darkness	Time Phrase
	will be many;	
	all that comes is *hebel*	Conclusion
11.9-10	*Rejoice*	Theme A
	(in your youth... in	Time Phrase
	the days of your youth	
	for youth...is *hebel*	Conclusion

(1975), pp. 519-31. M. Gilbert, 'La description de la vieillesse en Qohelet XII, 7,
est-elle allegorique?' in J.A. Emerton (ed.), *Congress Volume. Vienna 1980*
(VTSup, 32; Leiden: Brill, 1981), pp. 96-109; Ogden, 'Qoheleth XI 7–XII 8:
Qoheleth's Summons to Enjoyment and Reflection', *VT* 34 (1984), pp. 27-38;
Crenshaw, 'Youth and Old Age in Qoheleth', *HAR* 10 (1986), pp. 1-13; Fox,
'Aging and Death in Qohelet 12', *JSOT* (1988), pp. 55-77.
    1.   The authenticity of 11.9b will be defended in Chapter 5.
    2.   Ogden, 'Qoheleth XI 7–XII 8', pp. 29-30. I would only add at this point that
the 'darkness' of 11.8 is also repeated in the darkness of 12.2, 3, extending the
rhetorical hegemony of 11.8 even further.

12.1	*Remember*	Theme A
	in the days of your youth	Time Phrase
	before...	
12.2	before...	
12.6	before...	
12.8	*hăbēl hăbălîm*...all is	Conclusion
	hebel	

His outline effectively reveals the line of Qoheleth's reasoning: enjoy life now, yet at the same time reflect 'upon its significance under the shadow of death'.[1] Actually, this shadow of death is what tutors us toward an immediate and full enjoyment of life. Here again we see death walking freely with Qoheleth, always making its presence known to ensure a sober, but not always somber assessment of life.

Another large section of Ecclesiastes is devoted to an analysis of one's enjoyment of property. By employing typical Hebraic techniques for cohesion in 5.10–6.9 (parallel and chiastic structures), Qoheleth clearly explains the pleasures, yet limitations of property.[2] In one of these parallel developments throughout the passage, four thematic concerns are repeated in sequence at three different times. Like the pattern above, where 11.8 determined the structure of 11.9–12.8, here, the introductory verses (5.10-12) outline what follows it.

a. The wealthy—lovers of money (5.10a)
b.   Temporary wealth—even this is breath (5.10b)
           —its consumers increase (5.11a)
c. So, what advantage? (5.11b)
d.   Advantage = contentment—pleasure of the eyes (5.11c)
           pleasant sleep (5.12)

a. The wealthy—preserved wealth (5.13)
b.   Temporary wealth—wealth is lost (5.14)
c. So, what advantage? (5.16)
d.   Advantage = contentment—eat, drink, and enjoy labor—5.18

a. The wealthy—gift of riches (6.2a)
b.   Temporary wealth—given to another (6.2b)
c. So, what advantage? (6.8)
d.   Advantage = contentment—pleasure of the eyes (6.9)

1.   Ogden, 'Qoheleth XI 7–XII 8', p. 38.
2.   For a complete description of the structure of this passage see Fredericks, 'Chiasm and Parallel Structure in Qoheleth 5.9–6.9', *JBL* 108 (1989), pp. 17-35. The impermanence of property can be a matter of justice too. This I will return to in Chapter 5.

In this development, 5.10-12 compactly establishes the premises and conclusions that are to be found in the two more expansive sections that follow. The reasons for 'temporary wealth' are described variously: 5.11—the consumers of one's wealth increase in proportion to one's income; 5.14—the riches are said vaguely to be lost in an unfortunate way; 6.2—the wealth of one is given to a stranger (cf. Ps. 39.6). Yet the advantage of pleasure is offered uniformly by Qoheleth, in spite of annoyances of these sorts. As long as one can enjoy his property, even if only by viewing it and being satisfied with the sight of it, this is *some* advantage (5.11c). What the eyes see and enjoy is preferable to what the soul only seeks; yet again, it is only temporary (*hebel*, 6.9). Though some may spend life in darkness with a bitter and sick heart (5.16), others will wring all the pleasure available from life regardless of its relative rarity (5.18).

The issue of temporary property is part of a second parallel development in this same passage.

a. There is an evil (5.12a)
    i   riches possessed (5.12b)
    ii   riches lost (5.13a)
b.   Begetting offspring (5.13b)
    i   having nothing (5.13c)
    ii   coming and going (5.14, 15a)
c. What advantage from toil? (5.15b)
    i   no satisfaction (5.16)
    ii   contentment (5.17-19b)

a. There is an evil (6.1)
    i   riches possessed (6.2a)
    ii   riches lost (6.2a)
b.   Begetting offspring (6.3a,
    i   having nothing (6.3b)
    ii   coming and going (6.4, 5)
c. What advantage from toil? (6.7, 8)
    i   no satisfaction (6.7b)
    ii   contentment (6.9)

Though the parallel structure is built and maintained with some different components than in the first parallel, the destination of the arguments is identical. It is unfortunate that wealth can be lost, especially when offspring can complicate the picture. And though one's fathering children only ends in his replacement on the earth, and though *complete* satisfaction is not the advantage to toil, one is still expected to be content with the pleasure available at any fleeting moment. Because property is temporary in many cases, one's enjoyment in life from the material benefits of labor can only inexcusably be ignored. No one is promised endless wealth, hence the passage closes with a guarded recommendation to enjoy the possessions that one can see *currently*. Like the will of the wind, and like breath itself, they had better be enjoyed now and should not be counted on indefinitely (6.9).

The most elaborate arrangement in 5.10–6.9 is a twelve tone chiasm.

5.10		a. Limited satisfaction from possessions
		b. Brevity of possessions (*hebel*)
11	A	c. What advantage?
		d. Enjoy what is in sight
12		e. The common man
		f. More rest
14		g. Begetting offspring
15-16	B	h. Coming and going
17		i. In darkness
18		j. Matter seen as good
19	C	k. Gift of wealth enjoyed
		l. This is a gift
6.1		j. Matter seen as evil
2	C^1	k. Gift of wealth lost
		l. This is breath
3		g. Begetting offspring
4	B^1	h. Coming and going
		i. In darkness
5		f. More rest
7		a. Limited satisfaction from possessions
8		c. What advantage?
	A^1	e. The common man
9		d. Enjoy what is in sight
		b. Brevity of possessions

In their central and pivotal position, CC^1 accent the cause of all events, namely the sovereign will of an unpredictable God. This theology is basic to Ecclesiastes (3.11, 14; 7.13, 14; 8.16, 17; 11.5) and is a reason given by many commentators for the apparent scepticism and cynicism in the book. In this case the sovereignty of God is seen in his choice to allow or not to allow one to enjoy his gift of great wealth. Thus the pleasures of wealth can entail certain frustrations, and again we have an incentive to enjoy life while possible.

These structural designs in 5.10–6.9 lead us to refine further our description of the purpose of the passage. Yes, wealth can be frustrating in its coming and going, but between our own coming and going there are true blessings available from God, including enjoying those possessions to some extent. At least in conjunction with the theme of the tentative value of wealth, there should be equal appreciation for the positive theme of enjoyment by all those who are enabled by the will of an absolutely sovereign God.

The third extensive discourse on pleasure and its brevity is found at the start of Qoheleth's philosophical search for wisdom and folly.[1] The first hypothesis is that pleasure is profitable, and he conveniently includes his conclusion early in his introduction of the search:

> I said to myself, 'Come now, I will make a test of pleasure; enjoy yourself'. But behold this also was temporary (breath). I said of laughter, 'It is mad', but of pleasure, 'What does it do?' (2.1, 2).

Notice laughter is madness, as we might expect to hear from him, given his repulsion of frivolity (7.2-6). But *pleasure*, now *its* results are questioned only rhetorically. Rather than implying a negative response immediately, he raises the question of the advantage of pleasure without the onus of association with superficial mirth. Pleasure should not be dismissed as valueless at the start, especially since there is a sustained and positive tone behind this itemization of accomplishments. This unit ends with the pleasant memory of the joy entailed in these pursuits (2.10), as well as his superiority over predecessors due to the advantage of wisdom (2.9, 12-14).[2] Admittedly, the advantage of pleasure has its limitations, as we have seen clearly before, but a serious reflection on two ostensibly contradictory statements will yield a synthesis that is definitely a candidate for the very theme of Ecclesiastes.

---

1. Crenshaw sees this survey itself to be endangered by brevity, 'The second infinitive, *wĕle'ĕhōz* (to grasp, hold on to), suggests the fleeting nature of sensual pleasure. Qoheleth latches on to folly…for a sustained period so that his judgment will not be skewed by the brevity of the test' (*Ecclesiastes*, p. 78).

2. His phrasing, *'ap…'āmdā* (even more…stood), magnifies the role of wisdom as it prevails over mirth, and sustains him through his search for wisdom.

And whatever my eyes desired I did not keep from them; I kept my heart from no pleasure, for my heart found pleasure in all my toil. Then I considered all that my hands had done and the toil I had spent doing it, and behold, all was temporary and like the will of the wind, so there was no profit under the sun (2.10, 11).

As we saw earlier in Chapter 3, when Qoheleth looks ahead at exactly how fleeting his achievements really are (2.14-23), he blurts out that there is 'no profit', since they were only breath. There is a reward of pleasure in one's labor (in what other terms could you describe a gift of God? [2.24-26; 3.12, 13; 5.19, 20]), but there is no *lasting* profit—the very conclusion anticipated back in 2.1; pleasure and enjoyment are only temporary.

The amassing of property, experiences, pleasures and otherwise that Qoheleth recounts in 2.4-8 is not only expressed in message but medium as well. As he expands his list of accomplishments in this passage, he simultaneously expands the syntactical units used to state those accomplishments. Of course the proof of this lies ultimately in the original Hebrew which builds a gradual lengthening in phrases measured by syllable counts. It might be simplistically reproduced as follows:

	Translation	Hebrew Syllables	Acquisitions as Direct Objects
4a	I expanded my works.	6	1
b	I built houses for myself.	6	1
c	I planted vineyards for myself.	7	1
5a	I constructed gardens and parks for myself.	10	1
b	I planted in them trees of all fruits.	23	1
6	I constructed pools for myself from which to water the forest of sprouting trees.	22	1
7a	I acquired male servants and female servants, and they bore more servants for me.	16	2
b	I possessed more property in herds and flocks than all my predecessors in Jerusalem.	24	2

| 8a | I also amassed for myself silver and gold and the treasures of kings, and provinces. | 21 | 4 |
| b | I acquired for myself male singers and female singers, and the delight of sons of men, many women. | 24 | 4 |

The syntactical structures grow systematically by and large, with some momentary setback in the number of syllables. The number of objects indicating the achievements and acquisitions ebb and flow toward conjunctive strings of as many as four 'and' clauses. Therefore the style itself pictures building and compiling, matching the pursuits of Qoheleth, who selects those that are clearly pleasurable as opposed to primarily functional, or utilitarian: palaces, gardens, orchards, servants, land, money, music and mistresses.

His elation voiced in 2.10 fades into the realism of 2.11, which in turn deteriorates into the depression of 2.14b-23. In spite of his efforts that brought enjoyment, efforts even guided by wisdom, their transitoriness prove too much to bear at a weak point in his quest. His strongest emotions are vented in this latter passage, though they are soothed by the consolations of 2.24-26.

The transitory nature of royal privilege and achievements is also noted by Qoheleth in reference to meteoric popularity. In a previous chapter I outlined Qoheleth's low estimation of collective recall. No less than five texts deal with the forgotten efforts of any individual. Apart from two neutral statements on the matter (1.11; 9.5), being forgotten can be a deplorable injustice to the wise (2.15, 16; 9.14, 15). In a further example of the latter situation, Qoheleth addresses popularity directly in his comparison of the foolish king and the wise lad:

> Better is a poor and wise youth than an old and foolish king, who will no longer take advice; even though he had gone from prison to the throne or in his own kingdom had been born poor. I saw all the living who move about under the sun, as well as that youth who was to stand in his place; there was no end to all the people; he was over all of them. Yet those who will come later will not rejoice in him. Surely this also is temporary and like the wind's desire (4.13-16).

Here, similar to the scenario in 9.14, 15, the wise person is initially poor and eventually forgotten, as he too is replaced by a second lad.[1]

---

1. Some see only two successive kings in this passage. However, Qoheleth

The fickle faithfulness of supporters is yet another frustration to one's aspirations to happiness; if ever obtained in the first place, the pleasures of popularity are to be cherished while the moment holds them. As Qoheleth universalizes later, 'the dead do not know anything, *nor* have they *any longer* (wĕ'ēn-'ôd) any reward, but the memory of them is lost' (9.5). The transience of one's reward is assured by the forgetfulness of others.

Qoheleth has run another thematic thread throughout his speech, from beginning to end; this time the concern is pleasure. Yet its consistent role as an answer to the frustrations and fatigue of strenuous labor present it as the most positive theme, if not the real point of the whole matter for Qoheleth. Since pleasure is too brief, being only breath, one's enjoyment should be an urgent, wholehearted objective in life.

makes his point whether he is in fact referring to two or three kings. Yet the point is intensified if we take 'the second lad' to refer to exactly that, a second *lad*. Since the only *lad* mentioned is the one who succeeds the aged king, a second lad probably refers to a third character in the scenario. For a survey of suggested historical allusions here see, Fredericks, *Qoheleth's Language*, pp. 4-5. I take it to be merely stereotypical, as are the rest of Qoheleth's political vignettes and allusions.

Chapter 5

TRANSIENT TRAGEDIES

Man that is born of woman is of few days, and full of trouble.
He comes forth like a flower, and withers;
He flees like a shadow, and continues not.

Job 14.1, 2

No one is aware of life's tragedies and injustices more than Qoheleth, and regardless how a person may have become insulated from the tragic status of humanity, one is without excuse for leaving Ecclesiastes unmoved or impassive. We have observed with Qoheleth how temporary are both the advantages of wise, strenuous labor and its fruit, which are to be enjoyed while possible. The evanescence of life and its experiences is troublesome enough, but to highlight the rest of life's miseries in conjunction with these disappointments could be overwhelming if it were not for his consolations strung along the way, designed to assist us in coping with transience. The balance of life's miseries will be our concern now as we view them through the empathy of Qoheleth, who for our bitter convenience, concentrates so many of life's ills in such a small space. Our eyes are not only filled with scenes of evil, adversity and woe, but what little room is left in them is moist with tears of sympathy for a world cursed and struggling to subsist on a few meager and rationed staples of human dignity and hope. Simply a survey of the gloomy vocabulary of Qoheleth shows his sensitivity toward this world: toil, tragedy, tears and troubles; drunkenness, darkness, dangers and death; mistakes, madness, miscarriages and mourning; wickedness, weariness, weeping and war; anger, arrogance and affliction; sleeplessness, sickness and sin; folly and failing bodies; cursing and killing; and pains, oppression, hatred, jealousy, laziness, entrapments and bribery; as well as various ways of expressing poor leadership and injustice, and loss of property. Such is the fabric of Ecclesiastes, but when this realism is coupled with the maxim, 'all is temporary', we are offered some comfort.

The fallow ground of the poor yields much food,
    but it is swept away through injustice (Prov. 13.23).

But for Qoheleth, regardless through which door riches depart, 'profitlessness' in life is partially due to the fact that as one is born with nothing, one dies taking nothing (5.14, 16).

Consequently, to labor in life and not find happiness and contentment is problem enough. But to add tragedy to itself, one is caught unaware when it does come, with no warning or preparation, 'ensnared at an evil time, when it suddenly falls on them'; 'anything awaits him'; 'you do not know what misfortune may occur on earth' (9.12, 1; 11.2). Such misfortune may loom in the dangerous everyday labor of the workman. Digging pits, quarrying stones, cutting trees are not only exhausting, gruelling toil, but provide a perpetual subliminal stress in their precariousness (10.8-10). Between the extremes of possible times of death, whether as a stillborn (6.3-6), or after a long life of the decrepit (12.1-6), the ever-threatening uncertainty of life and its shattering contents can eat away at whatever *shalom* one is blessed with.

Qoheleth recognizes that grief to the point of 'sickness' or 'pain' is common in life. It might come through the loss of property (5.13, 16; 6.2), but more generally, the bare awareness of the wretched conditions of this world, and the ominous tasks and failings of humanity bring about intense pain to the soul: 'in much wisdom is much grief, and he who increases knowledge increases sorrow' (1.18; cf. 2.23). 'Darkness' can dim any light in life, oppressing the soul and its efforts with grief, much vexation, sickness and resentment' (5.17; 6.4; 11.8; 12.2, 3). Sleeplessness is the result of grief and anxiety, 'all his days are full of pain, and his work is a vexation; even in night his mind does not rest' (2.23; cf. 1.18; 5.12). Even 'hatred' of one's situation practically can be excused as an initial response to a renewed realism about life (2.17, 18): 'So I hated life because what is done under the sun was grievous to me'.

Yet Qoheleth observes that hatred is not only directed toward circumstances but also toward other people (9.1, 6) and is expressed in various rancorous ways. Prov. 18.23 regrets the fact that,

The poor man utters supplications,
    But the rich man answers roughly.

Qoheleth concurs,

> I saw the tears of the oppressed and they had no one to comfort them
> (4.1).

> Man lords it over man to his hurt (8.9; cf. 5.8; 7.7).

'Jealousy' and 'rivalry' (4.4; 9.6), 'arrogance' (7.8), 'cursing' (7.21, 22; 10.20), are all common elements in the day's routine of human abuse. These daily vulgarities are epitomized in declarations of war, and in four instances Qoheleth addresses this topic explicitly. Certainly there is a time for it (3.8), there is even little hope for exemption from it and its effects for the individual (8.8); victory can be evasive and frustrating to one's expectations (9.11), not even bringing wealth or honor to those responsible for its success (9.11, 14ff.). It is no wonder, given the hatred and brutality in human relations, that 'tears' (4.1), 'weeping' (3.4) and 'mourning' (3.4; 7.2, 4; 12.5) play such an important role in Qoheleth's account of life.

Moral 'evil', 'wickedness' and 'sin', flourish on earth and are the root of most problems, including those listed above. With this vocabulary, Qoheleth describes further the failings of humanity; irreverence (5.1; 9.2) rebellion (8.3), adultery (7.26), and empty chatter (10.13), bribery (7.7), drunkenness (10.17), and laziness (4.5; 10.18), complete his logging of perversity that adds to the decadence of any society.

Rampant folly and madness, which he meets immediately at the outset of his search for the valuable and valueless aspects of life, will distress the wise (1.17; 2.2, 12; 7.7, 25; 9.3; 10.13). The fool walks in darkness (2.14), is slack (4.5), sacrifices meaninglessly (5.1), prattles (5.3, 12), dreams (5.3, 7), frivols (7.4, 5), cackles (7.6) and rages (7.9). Unbearable as it is to have to tolerate fools in common places, one must also endure under their leadership as kings (4.13; 10.5, 16, 17), judges (3.16; cf. 8.11), and princes (10.5-7). In regard to foolish leadership Qoheleth again agrees with Proverbs:

> It is not fitting for a fool to live in luxury,
>   much less for a slave to rule over princes (Prov. 19.10).

> There is an evil which I have seen under the sun, as it were an error proceeding from the ruler; folly is set in many high places, while rich men sit in a low place. I have seen slaves on horses, and princes walking on foot like slaves (Eccl. 10.5-7).

But in regard to wickedness in general, he agrees with a much more ancient Egyptian.

> To whom can I speak today?
> Gentleness has perished
> And the violent man has come down on everyone.
>
> To whom can I speak today?
> Men are contented with evil
> And goodness is neglected everywhere...
>
> To whom can I speak today?
> Hearts are rapacious
> And there is no man's heart in which one can trust.
>
> To whom can I speak today?
> There are no just persons
> And the land is left over to the doers of wrong.[1]

Surely there is not a righteous man on earth who does good and never sins (Eccl. 7.20; cf. 1 Kgs 8.46).

Because sentence against an evil deed is not executed speedily, the heart of the sons of men is fully set to do evil (Eccl. 8.11).

The hearts of men are full of evil, and madness is in their hearts while they live, and after that they go to the dead (Eccl. 9.3).

Now, coping with a life punctuated with these and endless other ills becomes an art, the art of wisdom. One of the first skills advised by Qoheleth is appropriate resignation to those events that are beyond one's control—problems may need only to be tolerated. For example, the sovereign will of a king may be so invincible that effective resistance would be impossible (8.3-8). Having no control over a successor, nor over forgetfulness, renders fretting about the destiny of one's achievements fruitless (2.16, 18, 19). Furthermore, folly at times is just too overpowering to counteract (9.18; 10.1). Ambushes by treachery and disaster leave one vulnerable and defenseless (9.11, 12). Even though resignation is prescribed in these cases, cynicism is not. We have already seen that the recurrent theme to enjoy life is made in full realization, even direct mitigation of these types of misfortune. In addition, such resignation for Qoheleth is nothing less

---

1. Faulkner, 'The Man who Was Tired of Life', pp. 28, 29. Yet the Egyptian, Ipu-wer, complains of the inversion of roles too; *ANET*, pp. 441-42.

than a theological necessity since it acknowledges God's sovereign will
which is not always known, much less alterable.

> Consider the work of God, who can make straight what he has made
> crooked? In the day of prosperity be joyful, and in the day of adversity
> consider; God has made the one as well as the other, so that man may not
> find out anything that will be after him (7.13, 14).
>
> But all this I laid to heart, examining it all, how the righteous and the wise
> and their deeds are in the hand of God; whether it is love or hate, man
> does not know (9.1; cf. 3.14; 6.10).

Yet resignation is hardly the only response; many of life's afflictions (itemized in Chapter 3) are either preventable or curable.
Qoheleth gives many instructions about anticipating and answering
afflictions wisely. For instance, both excessive wickedness and
industriousness are destructive—be realistic! (7.16-18). Fuming is
unnecessary—overcome it! (7.9; 8.1, 3; 10.4). Reckless and
unprofessional procedure may end in calamity—be careful! (10.8-11).
Lax administration of affairs encourages evil—be demanding! (5.8, 9;
8.11; 10.16-18). Uncertainties in life can impoverish one—be
diversified and diligent! (11.1-6). One who is stronger and threatening
may be about to destroy you—get help! (4.12).

Moreover, a greater wisdom is shown when one considers the
temporality of all things, including tragedies of all sorts, and *then* acts
accordingly. Three scenarios along these lines are presented within
administrative settings. First, a king's decree may not be reversible,
but the effects may be temporary, and a timely and apt response could
eventually relieve the burden (8.2-6): 'every matter has *a* (proper)
time and way...' Secondly, the proper time for appropriate action
against evil is fleeting, and must be taken advantage of quickly
(*mehēr*) while the wicked rampage (8.11). And thirdly, if a ruler is
riled, his temper's peak should be borne with composure for it will
subside in time (10.4; cf. Prov. 15.1). In fact, Qoheleth prescribes that
demeanor which depends precisely on the transience of annoyances,
and even tragedies—patience. He concludes most generally in 7.8,

> Better is the end of a thing than its beginning;
> and the patient in spirit is better than the proud in spirit.

This is not only his advice in areas of anger with fools and others, but
anger about disappointing realities overall (7.10, 13, 14).

Finally, there is no greater malady for Qoheleth than inversions in justice, where retribution is ironic, and rewards and penalties seem misdirected. The irritating leadership and justice of the wicked and fools were noted above already, but justice is not always found in life in general either.

There is a righteous man who perishes in his righteousness, and there is a wicked man who prolongs his life in his evil doing (7.14b).

There are righteous men to whom it happens according to the deeds of the wicked, and there are wicked men to whom it happens according to the deeds of the righteous (8.14b).

The race is not to the swift, nor the battle to the strong, nor bread to the wise, nor riches to the intelligent, nor favor to the men of skill; but time and chance happen to them all (9.11).

The poor man's wisdom is despised, and his words are not heeded…one sinner destroys much good…a little folly outweighs wisdom and honor (9.16, 18; 10.1).

Moreover, if justice is not seen readily in life, death seems to nullify any final possibility of fair retribution.

One fate comes to all, to the righteous and the wicked, to the good and the evil, to the clean and the unclean, to him who sacrifices and to him who does not sacrifice. As is the good man, so is the sinner; and he who swears is as he who shuns an oath. This is an evil in all that is done under the sun, that one fate comes to all (9.2, 3a).

As noted in the first chapter of this volume, much of Qoheleth's supposed cynicism is attributed to a desperate resignation to this frequent inversion of justice. Crüsemann evaluated Ecclesiastes in this light, representing many others.

A basic presupposition of Koheleth's thinking is that there is no connection between what human beings do and how they fare. This means, of course, that the world and the God who acts in it are completely impenetrable, unpredictable, and unjust.[1]

These ironic observations by Qoheleth are not unique to him; simply to question divine retribution certainly was not anathema outside of Ecclesiastes, since any lucid mind inevitably will raise the same

---

1. Crüsemann, 'The Unchangeable World', pp. 59-60. He gives an excellent presentation of this main-line view of Ecclesiastes, uniquely integrating the interpretation with socio-economic and political antecedents.

questions. Usually the matter does not rest there, however, but is answered with the advice to be patient and persevere until God's absolute justice is accomplished. For instance, frequent grievances about the success of the wicked are found in the *psalms*, but there is solace in the transience of the wicked's perpetuity and prosperity, for example:

> In the pride of his countenance the wicked does not seek him;
>> all his thoughts are, 'There is no God'.
> His ways prosper at all times; thy judgments are on high, out of his sight;
>> as for all his foes, he puffs at them...
> O Lord, thou wilt hear the desire of the meek;
>> thou wilt strengthen their heart, thou wilt incline thine ear
> to do justice to the fatherless, and the oppressed,
>> so that man who is of the earth may strike terror no more (Ps. 10.4,
>> 5, 17, 18).

> For I was envious of the arrogant,
>> when I saw the prosperity of the wicked.
> For they have no pangs;
>> their bodies are sound and sleek...
> Truly thou dost set them in slippery places;
>> thou dost make them fall to ruin.
> How they are destroyed in a moment,
>> swept away utterly by terrors (Ps. 73.3, 4, 18, 19).

> The dull man cannot know,
>> the stupid cannot understand this:
> that though the wicked sprout like grass and all evil doers flourish,
> they are doomed to destruction for ever,
>> but thou, O Lord, art on high for ever (Ps. 92.6-8 cf. Pss. 13, 37, 49,
>> 52, 55, 64, 89, 94).

The *prophets* enquire about and resolve the issue as well—

> Why does the way of the wicked prosper? Why do all who are treacherous thrive? Thus says the Lord concerning all my evil neighbors who touch the heritage which I have given my people Israel to inherit: 'Behold, I will pluck them up from their land, and I will pluck up the house of Judah from among them. And after I have plucked them up I will have compassion on them, and I will bring them again each to his heritage and each to his land (Jer. 12.1b, 14, 15).

> Why dost thou make me see wrongs
>> and look upon trouble?
> Destruction and violence are before me;
>> strife and contention arise.

So the law is slacked
  and justice never goes forth.
For the wicked surround the righteous,
  so justice goes forth perverted.
'Woe to him who heaps up what is not his own—for how long?
  and loads himself with pledges!'
Will not your debtors suddenly arise,
  and those awake who will make you tremble?
Then you will be booty for them.
Because you have plundered many nations,
  all the remnant of the peoples will plunder you ...(Hab. 1.3, 4;
    2.6b-8a).

As expected, Proverbs consistently encourages trust in God's eventual justice:

Fret not yourself because of evil-doers,
  and be not envious of the wicked;
for the evil man has no future;
  the lamp of the wicked will be put out (Prov. 24.19, 20).[1]

The problem posed in Hebrew theology concerning the apparent success of the wicked therefore, is frequently answered by the *temporality* of that prosperity, terminated by the just judgment of God. This should include Ecclesiastes as well, where the same sentiment is found *prima facie*, for example:

Moreover I saw under the sun that in the place of justice there was wickedness, and in the place of righteousness there was wickedness. I said in my heart, 'God will judge the righteous and the wicked, for he has appointed a time for every matter and for every work' (3.16, 17).

Various extraordinary measures have been taken to define the function and even authenticity of statements such as this which affirm just retribution (see also, 2.26; 8.12, 13; 11.9). One certainly must struggle to some extent with such orthodoxy in a book considered to be agnostic in epistemology and fatalistic in ethics.[2]

Commentators in as diverse times and places as Barton and Lauha attribute such passages to a glossator bent on making Ecclesiastes look

---

1.   Other examples: 10.25, 27; 11.5; 12.7; 13.22; 14.11, 32; 24.15, 26; 29.16.

2.   For an excellent survey of how inconsistencies in Qoheleth have been handled, including retribution, see Crenshaw, 'Qoheleth in Current Research', *HAR* 7 (1984), pp. 43-51.

theologically acceptable.[1] For instance, a warning found in the midst of the commendations of pleasure in 11.7-10 is ejected as inconsistent with their readings of Qoheleth's message:

> 'But know that for all these things God will bring you to judgment' (11.9b).

Such a direct statement about conventional justice from God flies in the face of an interpretation of Ecclesiastes that is commonly summarized, by 'all is vanity'. On the other hand, Gordis would retain such a statement, suggesting the basis for such judgment of God to be whether the person enjoyed God's gifts or whether those gifts were despised. There would not be any judgment on the basis of a person's overall righteousness or unrighteousness.[2] Rather than hypothesize any glossator in the pertinent passages, Gordis and others would retain other orthodox statements about retribution as a part of Ecclesiastes, but only as quotations by Qoheleth of conventional wisdom which were erroneous and should be rejected and substituted with a more sceptical conclusion.[3] So, for instance, 3.17 quoted above is not really Qoheleth's solution to the injustices of 3.16, but 'the shadowy doctrine of retribution in another world, which he dismisses with a shrug of the shoulders'.[4] However, there are still others who would not dismiss these orthodox moments as later glosses or maxims to be defrocked, but as Qoheleth's sincere conviction about a just God and his delayed retribution;[5] justice is a matter of time.

Gordis also resorts to describing Qoheleth's use of ethical language as 'unconventional': for instance, it is suggested that where the sage uses 'sinner' he really means the 'fool, one who misses the right path', that is, missing the joy available from God.[6] Crenshaw also remolds the meaning for 'sinner' to be, 'unfortunate, unlucky'.[7] Whether the

---

1.   Barton, *Ecclesiastes*, pp. 43-46; Lauha, *Kohelet*, pp. 4-7.

2.   Gordis, *Koheleth*, pp. 93-94, 336, 227.

3.   Gordis argues extensively for the authenticity of Ecclesiastes by the quotation theory, *Koheleth*, pp. 95-108. Also Scott, *Proverbs, Ecclesiastes*, e.g. pp. 223, 225.

4.   Gordis, *Koheleth*, pp. 158-59, 234-35.

5.   E.g. Whybray, 'Joy', pp. 90, 96; Eaton, *Ecclesiastes*, pp. 84-85; Ogden, *Qoheleth*, pp. 59-60; Fox, *Qohelet and his Contradictions* (JSOTSup, 71; Sheffield: Almond Press, 1989), pp. 121-50, 279.

6.   Gordis, *Koheleth*, pp. 227-28, 282.

7.   Crenshaw, *Ecclesiastes*, p. 90: 'For Qoheleth *ḥôṭe'* almost retains its original neutral connotation of errant, missing the mark'. Also, p. 146.

meaning was quite this neutral for Qoheleth is not an excuse even as
far as Qoheleth himself is concerned, since a plea of 'mistake' will not
impress God, who considers such irresponsibility to be *sin* and worthy
of punishment (5.6; I will return to this presently). With such
redefinitions of typically moral vocabulary, statements that appear to
encourage righteousness, and speak of impending judgment are sup-
posedly redirected; for example, 2.26, and 7.26:

> For to a man who pleases him, God gives wisdom, knowledge, and joy;
> but to the *sinner* he gives the work of gathering and heaping, only to give
> to one who pleases God.

> And I found more bitter than death the woman whose heart is snares and
> nets, and whose hands are fetters; he who pleases God escapes her, but
> the *sinner* is taken by her.

However, the first reference has its perfect parallel in conventional
wisdom (Prov. 13.22),

> A good man leaves an inheritance to his children's children,
>   but the *sinner's* wealth is laid up for the righteous.

It is probable that the impermanence of personal property then is
recognized by Qoheleth to be not only a tragedy that anyone might
experience (2.18, 21), but also to be due to the retributive
prerogatives of God.

Furthermore, it is unnecessary to disallow passages such as these,
since they are in complete congruity with the obvious and inextricable
statements of classical wisdom that have been seen by most to be
authentic in Ecclesiastes, which are neither glosses nor conventional
platitudes to be discarded. Qoheleth's commendations of *wisdom* have
been highlighted earlier in detail, commendations that are built on
realistic expectations about God's sovereign timing and execution of
justice. In addition to commending wisdom, Qoheleth commends
righteousness explicitly, which is inseparable from wisdom in the
Hebrew wisdom literature. This in part is because of the implications
of righteousness. Earlier in this chapter we scanned his examples of
wickedness and folly. They include the cultic passage of ch. 5,
including vv. 1 and 6;

> Guard your steps when you go to the house of God; to draw near to listen
> is better than to offer the sacrifice of fools; for they do not know that they
> are *doing evil*...Let not your mouth lead you into sin, and do not say

> before the messenger that it was a mistake; why should God be angry at
> your voice, and destroy the work of your hands?

Divine retribution is firmly in Qoheleth's mind here. In addition, sin
is pervasive, 'Surely there is not a righteous man on earth who does
good and never *sins*' (7.20). Sin is destructive, 'Be not overly *wicked*,
neither be a fool; why should you die before your time?' (7.17). Sin
betrays the sinner, 'nor will *wickedness* deliver those who are given to
it' (8.8). No wonder Qoheleth encourages one 'to *do good*' (3.12).

> I know that there is nothing better for them than to be happy and *to do
> good* as long as they live.

That he is praising righteousness in this latter reference should be
clear enough. Though many would see the phrase *'asa tôb* to be parallel to the Greek *eû práttein*, 'to fare well', rather than a moral injunc-
tion,[1] it is paralleled most closely later in the very verses quoted
above in 5.1 and 7.20. In 5.1, the syntactical equivalent of 'to do good'
(*la'ăśôt tôb*) is found, that is, 'to do evil' (*la'ăśôt rā'*), where it undoubtedly expresses the opposite moral pole. And in 7.20, to 'do good'
(*ya'śeh-tôb*), and never sin, are moral opposites as well. Righteousness
is a theme in Ecclesiastes, where it is abundantly clear that to pursue
wickedness is playing with God's patience. It is curious that some will
admit Qoheleth's conviction of God's retribution in the cultic context
of 5.1-6, but not in other areas of life—an unnecessary and arbitrary
dichotomy that is conceivable, but by no means supportable from
Ecclesiastes itself. Explicit pronouncements of God's foreboding judgment found in 3.17 and 11.9, therefore, are fully in line with Qoheleth's
moral universe.

This is equally true for the longer passage on the subject in 8.12-14.
This is possibly the most critical text because from it one determines
an important key to the rest of Qoheleth's comments on retribution.

> Though a sinner does evil a hundred times and prolongs his life, yet I
> know that it will be well with those who fear God, because they fear

---

1. E.g. Braun, *Kohelet*, p. 54; Hertzberg, *Prediger*, p. 56. Because the Hebrew
phrase does mean 'do (moral) good' elsewhere in biblical Hebrew (Gen. 29.26,
Ps. 14.1, 34.15), and especially in Ecclesiastes itself, such a Hellenistic influence is
unlikely. Besides, others who accept that the phrase does mean 'fare well' in this
passage would see a biblical precedent in 2 Sam. 12.18, *'āśā rā'ā*, 'to do oneself
harm', where the meaning obviously is the opposite, negative result of a reflexive
act. See e.g. Loretz, *Qohelet*, p. 48.

before him; but it will not be well for the wicked, neither will he prolong his days like a shadow, because he does not fear before God. There is a *hevel* which takes place on earth, that there are righteous men to whom it happens according to the deeds of the wicked, and there are wicked men to whom it happens according to the deeds of the righteous. I said that this also is *hevel* (8.12-14).

A complication arises for many interpreters of this passage because of the clear statement of orthodoxy in vv. 12 and 13, followed by a so-called 'vanity', namely the inversion of justice to the wicked and righteous. This is a *non sequitur* for some, consequently it is dealt with in ways described earlier; that is, either 8.12, 13 is a gloss, or if its presence is due to Qoheleth, it was so only to be corrected by the sceptical conclusion of v. 14. However, if the meaning of *hevel* here is 'temporary', the alleged contradiction is removed and Qoheleth is placed squarely within the wisdom community's view of retribution that many feel he is disputing. In other words, the effort to expel ethical orthodoxy at almost every front in Ecclesiastes ends in many exotic theories made unnecessary simply by allowing *hevel* one of its proper biblical connotations. It is only a *temporary* situation that justice is not apparent, since 'neither will the wicked prolong his days like a shadow, because he does not fear before God.[1] Like some prophets and poets, Qoheleth is consoled by the fact that 'everything is temporary'. Psalm 49 concludes in the same manner:

Be not afraid when one becomes rich,
    when the glory of his house increases.
For when he dies he will carry nothing away;
    his glory will not go down after him.
Though, while he lives, he counts himself happy,
    and though a man gets praise when he does well for himself,
He will go to the generations of his fathers,
    who will never more see the light.
Man cannot abide in his pomp,
    he is like the beasts that perish.

---

1.   In an attempt to refute that this particular *hevel* means 'temporary' in 8.14, Fox employs an argument *reductio ad absurdum*: 'To call this situation "vaporous" gives no information about it; none of the qualities usually associated with vapors seem to apply. It is not 'transitory' or 'fleeting'—if it were, that would be all to the good' (*Hebel*, p. 412).

It is unnecessary to see Qoheleth as one who encourages fearing a God who is unpredictably unfair; instead he is one who advises reverence to a God who is predictably just, but within his own agenda and timing; 'fear God because he is wholly just and powerful'— precisely a theme of wisdom literature across the board. One can even go as far as to say that the conventional act-consequence conviction (you reap what you sow) is still a vital encouragement for Qoheleth. Not only does he commend righteousness, and warn against sin and God's negative judgment, but in a symmetrical way, he speaks of God's *blessings* to the righteous. The possible transfer of the sinner's property to the righteous mentioned in 2.26, was noted above. But that verse also adds that God will reward those in whom he delights with greater wisdom and knowledge, over and above the joy that is constantly spoken of as a solace in a tumultuous world. More generally, he observes that it does go well for those who fear God (8.12). In these very broad statements, Qoheleth echoes Proverbs in its bold generalizations. Certainly he is aware of the exceptional situations; in fact, it is precisely these that he moves on to in 8.13-15. If Ecclesiastes is indeed consistent with other wisdom literature in this regard, as well as more broadly, then the role of the book in the development of Hebrew theology and wisdom truly needs some degree of reassessment. Qoheleth's message assuredly is not identical to Proverbs, but he does not dismiss such ethical guidance as superfluous. He has so absorbed that conventional wisdom that he can now go on to dispel any unrealistic expectations and deal with the tragic exceptions to the rules of the Proverbial type of wisdom. This degree of qualification is an important part of the speech, but the observations, comments and refinements of this sort are not as extreme as to call them disagreements or contradictions. They are the reflections of a realist who wishes not to discard Hebrew theism, but feels pressed to address some of life's challenges to that theology.

Chapter 6

EVERYTHING IS BREATH!

Whatever men do does not last forever,
Mankind and their achievements alike come to an end.

A Mesopotamian Sage*

The enquiry in Chapter 1 emphasized what Qoheleth meant by
'everything is *breath (hevel)*'. In this final chapter an interesting question arises from reversing the emphasis: what does he mean by
'*everything (kōl)* is breath'? It is unlikely that he means 'everything'
in the absolute sense, since he continues only a few verses later, 'the
earth remains *forever*' (1.4), and later yet he says 'whatever God does
endures *forever*' (3.14).[1] Both of these statements reflect acts of the
creating God, which are in direct contrast to the temporary labors of
humanity. The task then is to review inductively the scope of everything that is temporary according to Qoheleth.[2] In the most general
way, this scope includes human life and its experiences, but those
experiences could be itemized further along the lines of (1) results of

---

* 'Counsels of a Pessimist', in W.L. Lambert, *Babylonian Wisdom Literature*
(Oxford: Clarendon Press, 1975), p. 109.
1.   Qoheleth obviously uses a restricted sense of 'everything' at times, for
instance in 7.15 where he claims to have seen 'everything' (*kōl*) in his brief life.
2.   Though Fox prefers the meaning 'absurd' for *hevel*, nonetheless he correctly
describes the challenge for all interpreters: '*Hebel* is applied to different types of
phenomena: beings, life or a part thereof, acts, and events...*Hebel* is most often
applied to situations or events in Qoheleth...The attempt to determine the meaning
of *hebel* in Qoheleth runs up against a special grammatical problem: it is frequently
difficult, sometimes virtually impossible, to identify the antecedents of the pronouns
[*zeh*] in the *hebel*-judgments. Thus, in particular cases it is uncertain what exactly is
being judged—a thing or action mentioned in the context, or the entire event or situation described' (*Hebel*, pp. 414-15).

one's efforts, (2) pleasure, and (3) tragedy. Actually, his most universal pronouncements of brevity are in the context of these different emphases. First, his introductory, 'Temporary, temporary; temporary, temporary; *total* temporariness', is followed by his thematic question about *toil* (1.2, 3, 14). Secondly, in 11.8 in the midst of commending pleasure, he warns, '*All* that comes is temporary'. Finally, after depicting graphically the demise of the *body* and its accomplishments, he concludes again, 'Temporary, temporary; *total* temporariness' (12.8).

Certainly Qoheleth agrees with the other Israelite and Middle Eastern sages who consider the temporality of life itself, and this is true regardless of one's understanding of *hevel*. Such an emphasis is found in 2.10–3.22, culminating in the comparison of the fleeting existence of both human and beast (3.19). To add urgency, Qoheleth warns that one's even shorter '*prime* of life' must be enjoyed while possible (11.10), for if joy is not found in any part of one's life, it would be better not to even reach the prime of life, but rather to pass into the darkness as a stillborn (6.4). Once death's inevitability and finality is firmly in mind, Qoheleth uses the truth of life's brevity as a natural qualification of living, speaking in terms of 'the few days of *his* fleeting life' (6.12), 'in *my* fleeting days' (7.15), 'every day of *your* fleeting life' (9.9—twice).

Again, like other ancient sages and poets Qoheleth emphasizes human transience; but he wants to say much more. His purpose is to extend the relevance of transience to *everything* in this one presentation. However, he does limit the scope of his conclusions about his observations explicitly, by constantly qualifying them through three Hebrew equivalents of our concept of 'visible reality'. These phrases identify the parameters of his search and observations of 'everything': 'under the sun' (nearly 30 times); 'under heaven' (three times); and 'on the earth' (six times). This is the scope of his observation and experiences, and he has resigned himself to knowing or discovering nothing else. A conclusion of his is that all which he does see in reality, or 'under the sun', is temporary (unless of course, it is a creation of God). In a less direct way, he anticipates the observations of a later theologian: 'For things that are seen are transient, but the things that are unseen are eternal' (2 Cor. 4.18). Qoheleth is aware of both realms too, the transient and the eternal. All that he sees is fleeting, though he affirms the eternal as the gift of God, put in man's heart (3.11).

More often than any other one experience, Qoheleth's interest is in the evanescence of human labor and its result. This subject is concentrated in mainly three passages which have at least three *hevel* statements each. The most compact and concentrated section is 2.10-26, where the results of one's labor are, on seven occasions, expressed as only temporary (2.11, 15, 17, 19, 21, 23, 26). A little later in 4.4-8, the temporary value of toil is accented again, three times with *hevel* statements (4.4, 7, 8) and once with only a 'will of the wind' comparison (4.6). This section closes with a scenario of the temporary value of a solitary man's labor. Since its fruit cannot be transferred at death to a brother or son, its worth is available only as long as the lonely man lives himself. This is where Qoheleth comes closest to speaking about any futility in labor. Though *hevel* does not connote it here, the absence of pleasure in conjunction with *hevel*ness does leave one living a life of emptiness, where transitory and nontransferable labor of the man only intensifies his tragedy of an unsatisfied, unenjoyable life. A few verses later in a third section he returns to the fruit of wealth and the simple possessions gained from one's labor, and he ascribes brevity to them as well (5.10–6.9; 5.10, 6.2, 9). As Qoheleth scanned 'all' *works*, wisdom, madness and folly under the sun, he concluded that all were only temporary (1.14; 1.17[1]); this would include efforts through words themselves (6.11),[2] or merely those things associated with words (5.7).[3]

Though pleasures are a major consolation for Qoheleth, they still are only temporary as well. This is especially true for any odious mirth expressed by obnoxious laughter (2.1; 7.6), but unfortunately it is true for all pleasures, including even those that could be commendable. Nonetheless, the acceptable pleasures of youth are encouraged (11.10), in addition to the numerous delights Qoheleth speaks of elsewhere, including popularity and public support (4.16).

Fortunately, injustice is likewise impermanent, though he surely is

1. In addition to 4.6, 1.17 is the other case where 'will of the wind' is alone, without *hevel*.

2. One wonders whether 'matters' should not be preferred here over 'words'. However, the consensus is strongly in favor of 'words'.

3. This verse has had many solutions suggested for its problematic syntax. Consult the commentaries for the proposals and disagreements.

aware of its cruelty and pervasiveness (8.10,[1] 8.14, 14). The eventual termination of injustice amounts to some consolation for those who find their circumstances at least offensive, as well as for those who find their situation excruciating.

Transience and pleasure are realities that we have seen Qoheleth combine often, yet they come together no more forcefully and succintly than in the two sentences of 9.6, 7:

> Their love and their hate and their envy have already (*kĕbār*) perished, and they have no longer, forever (*'ên-lāhem 'ôd le'ôlām*) any share that is done under the sun. Go! Eat your bread with enjoyment, and drink your wine with a merry heart; for God has already approved what you do.

Though he affirms emphatically that all activities and their motivations are surely brief ('already'), and indeed final ('no longer, forever'), the encouraging and comforting words of Qoheleth should bring pleasure and delight to most. The central point of the wisdom literature as a whole is the *shalom* that comes from a successful management of one's personal life. That may not end in lasting 'profit' of any exorbitant amount, but it will lead to some contentment in life (e.g. Prov. 16.8, 17.1). Qoheleth agrees with his colleagues, that there are advantages: he speaks often of wisdom and the good that follows as the means and ends of toil which positively answers his initial question: 'What does man gain by all the toil at which he toils under the sun?' (1.3).

This study has suggested that the key word in Ecclesiastes means 'temporary' in most cases, as opposed to any more negative meanings like 'empty, futile, vain', etc. Supportive evidence from the whole of Ecclesiastes has been presented to show that apart from this specific word's use in the book, the brevities in life are a main concern of Qoheleth, whereas any vanity or absurdity in life is not a significant focus. Though life may in some cases be reduced to futility (4.7, 8), it in no way can be characterized as such for those who seek wisdom and joy.

Commentators who would take the more traditional and negative view of Ecclesiastes do accept the epilogue's description of Qoheleth as

---

1.   This is yet another verse where complications do obscure the meaning considerably. I suggest the following translation only tentatively: 'Then I saw the wicked buried; they used to go in and out of the holy place, but they were forgotten in the city where they had done such things. This too is temporary'.

a shepherd who sought to find 'delightful', or 'pleasing' (*ḥēpeṣ*[1]) words. This proposed reading of Ecclesiastes, where *hevel* means 'temporary', might make Qoheleth's attempt a bit more successful. Undoubtedly some will think Ecclesiastes has been sterilized with this reading, and that any sting of scepticism, agnosticism, pessimism or cynicism has been neutralised. Though this proposed understanding of the book does render it less embittered, that is only because the objective has been to see Ecclesiastes more coherently. The conclusion to the matter then is that Qoheleth's mystifying juggling of 'wisdom', 'toil', 'tragedy' and 'joy' is comprehended best by looking at the book from the perspective of transience *of* life, and *in* life.

On the other hand, one cannot deny that Qoheleth does spend more time on the dark side of life in his presentation than we find in a so-called 'conventional' book of wisdom such as Proverbs. He dwells on those aspects of life that *Proverbs* assumes but prefers not to highlight. This difference in emphasis perhaps has been overestimated in current assessments of Ecclesiastes' role in the history of Israel's thought. The 'crisis' that Qoheleth allegedly portrays, and which I have occasionally referred to earlier, is certainly less if *hevel* indeed does often mean 'temporary' in his speech. Consequently, the 'crisis' hypothesis is a paradigm that may need some significant modification. Unsurprisingly, there have been those who have recognized the roots of Qoheleth's clear realism in other biblical literature, though few would see the same degree of similarity that we are suggesting here.[2] Injustice, tragedy, oppression, and concerns about divine retribution, its existence or mere delay, is not peculiar to him. Limitations of one's knowledge about life and God's mind are also of course paralleled elsewhere, including Proverbs. If classical wisdom is caricatured as

1. Ecclesiastes uses *ḥēpeṣ* in two distinct ways: as 'matter, pursuit, activity' (3.1, 17; 8.6); and as 'delight, pleasure' (5.3; 12.1, 10). The delighting aspects of Qoheleth's words are of only an aesthetic, formal nature according to most commentators. This is of course a natural interpretation if the traditional, negative understanding of Ecclesiastes is held. But the delight may not simply be literary and aesthetic, but something more; it probably is meant to reflect the response of joy from one's whole being that Qoheleth so frequently prescribes in his speech, and which is a significant theme of the speech.

2. For a brief survey of such observations by recent scholars, see Fredericks, *Qoheleth's Language*, pp. 272-78. There it is argued that a possible earlier date for Ecclesiastes (eighth or seventh century) makes Qoheleth's less positive presentation of reality roughly concurrent with 'classical' wisdom.

flashing an insipid grin at the horrendous face of tortured humanity, Qoheleth might be viewed as an off-center malcontent in Israelite wisdom. But if Ecclesiastes is seen to be a more concentrated version of a realism that simply surfaces less often from the mind of more conventional wisdom writers, then we have a more accurate picture of Qoheleth as a sage and of his contribution to Israel's rich wisdom literature and culture.

The intent of this study has not been merely to itemize and discuss those aspects of life that Qoheleth emphasizes as temporary, but also to highlight his prescribed consolations and means of coping with brevities in life. For him, coping with transience in all its manifestations involves resignation to some degree. It should be a relief for the wise to know what potential success there is to any effort, and if it is nil, to be free to redirect one's time and energy. He speaks often of resignation to both God's sovereign will and to circumstances equally beyond one's control. For instance, the evils of death and the ailments and woes that precede it are evils, but some consolation is offered when Qoheleth indeed assures his readers that life's experiences are not arbitrary but determined by a God interested in timeliness and even the beauty of that timing, though neither may be perceivable. Or, the power of government, whether foolish or wise, can be too much for an individual to counteract. Or, at times injustice may reign, and neither the righteous nor the wicked may receive their due. But regardless of the calamities and complications of life, Qoheleth advises both patience and reverence for God nonetheless.

Yet resignation does not imply cynicism—for two very important reasons. Though God does have the world measured and cast, human responsibility is expected both in the use of *wisdom* and in accepting whatever *delights* one meets along the way. To apply wisdom skillfully is a way to achieve an advantage and profit in life, no matter how temporary it might be. The advantage of wisdom is that it gives success, and Ecclesiastes is replete with examples of those means of coping with transience which entail aggressive, wise and advantageous pursuits, as well as how to protect oneself astutely from those tragedies in life that could shorten those pursuits even more. Qoheleth does not wink at wisdom with a patronizing, condescending smile, nor does he demean it as worthless or vain. Rather, he honors it, and elevates it to the same height as the commendable goal of life that is encouraged elsewhere in the Hebrew biblical literature.

Finally, Qoheleth adds pleasure to the ways of coping with transience. Simple pleasures of eating, drinking, seeing the sun, sleeping soundly, dancing, laughter, and embracing are all to be enjoyed, though these experiences can be just as ephemeral as the rest of life's experiences. A pleasant life spent with one's husband or wife, love and peace in the family, or peace as a nation, are yet other joys. He also depends heavily on the joy of work, even strenuous labor, to counterbalance the pains of a fleeting world which consists only of moments. It is precisely within one's efforts that one discovers any advantage.

What advantage is there for the sons of men in their labors?

Qoheleth's answer to this is expressed both after his specific search in the early chapters and within his review of his life-long observations that constitute the rest of Ecclesiastes: any advantage in one's life and labors is to be found in wise efforts that end in individual success and that make possible any pleasurable moments that are still available in this ravaged world.

It is the glory of God to conceal a matter,
    but the glory of kings is to search things out
Prov. 25.2.

BIBLIOGRAPHY

Baltzer, K., 'Women and War in Qohelet 7.23–8.1a', *HTB* 80 (1987), pp. 127-32.

Barton, G.A., *The Book of Ecclesiastes* (ICC, Edinburgh, 1908).

Barucq, A., *Ecclesiastes* (Paris: Beauchesne, 1968).

Bauernfeind, O., 'mataiótēs', *TDNT* 4, pp. 519-20 (Grand Rapids, 1967).

Bertram, G., 'Herbräischer und griechischer Qohelet', *ZAW* 64 (1952), pp. 26-49.

Braun, R., *Kohelet und die frühellenistiche Popular Philosophie* (*BZAW*, 130; Berlin, 1973).

Brin, G., 'The Significance of the Form *mah-ttob*', *VT* 38 (1988), pp. 462-65.

Brindle, W.A., 'Righteousness and Wickedness in Ecclesiastes 7.15-18', *Andrews University Seminary Studies* 23 (1985), pp. 243-57.

Bruns, J.E., 'The Imagery of Eccles. 12.6a', *JBL* 84 (1965), pp. 428-30.

Burkitt, F.C., 'Is Ecclesiastes a Translation?', *JTS* (1921), pp. 22-28.

Chopineau, J., 'L'image de Qohelet dans l'exégèse contemporaine', *Revue d'historie et de philosophie religieuses* 59 (1979), pp. 595-603.

Craigie, P.C., *Psalms 1–50* (Waco: Word Books, 1983).

Crenshaw, J.L., 'Popular Questioning of the Justice of God in Ancient Israel', *ZAW* 82 (1970), pp. 380-95.

—'The Eternal Gospel', pp. 23-56 in J. Crenshaw and J. Willis (eds.), *Essays in Old Testament Ethics* (New York, 1974).

—'The Shadow of Death in Qoheleth', in J.G. Gammie *et al.* (eds.), *Israelite Wisdom* (Missoula, 1979).

—'Qoheleth in Ancient Research', *HAR* 7 (1984), pp. 41-56.

—'The Expression *mî vôdēaʿ* in the Hebrew Bible', *VT* 36 (1986), pp. 274-88.

—'Youth and Old Age in Qoheleth', *HAR* 10 (1986), pp. 1-13.

—*Ecclesiastes* (OTL; Philadelphia, 1987).

Crüsemann, F., 'The Unchangeable World: The "Crisis of Wisdom" in Koheleth', in W. Schotroff and W. Stegemann (eds.), *God of the Lowly* (Maryknoll, 1984), pp. 57-77. Trans. of *Dis unveranderbare Welt*, in *Der Gott der Kleine Leute* (Munich, 1979), pp. 80-104.

Dahood, M., 'Qoheleth and Recent Discoveries', *Bib* 39 (1958), pp. 302-18.

—review of O. Loretz' *Qohelet und der alte Orient*, *Bib* 46 (1964), pp. 234-36.

Donald, T., 'The Semantic Field of "Folly" in Proverbs, Job, Psalms, and Ecclesiastes', *VT* 13 (1963), pp. 285-92.

Driver, S.R., *An Introduction to the Literature of the Old Testament* (Edinburgh, 1913).

Dulin, R.Z., *A Crown of Glory: A Biblical View of Aging* (New York, 1988).

Eaton, M.A., *Ecclesiastes* (Leicester, 1983).

Eissfeldt, D., 'Alles Ding währt seine Zeit: Qoh 3.1-14', in A. Kuschke *et al.* (eds.), *Archäologie und Altes Testament festschrift für Kurt Galling* (Tübingen, 1970), pp. 69-74.

Ellermeier, F., 'Das Verbum *ḥûš* in Koh. 2:25', *ZAW* 75 (1963), pp. 197-217.

—'Die Entmachung der Weisheit in Denken Qohelets: Zu Text und Auslegung von Qoh. 6:7-9', *ZTK* 60 (1963), pp. 1-20.

—*Qohelet*, Teil I, Abschnitt 1, Herzberg, 1967.

Faulkner, R.O., 'The Man who Was Tired of Life', *JEA* 42 (1956), pp. 21-40.

Foresti, F., ' *'āmāl* in Koheleth: "Toil" or "Profit"', *ETL* 31 (1980), pp. 415-30.

Forman, C., 'The Pessimism of Ecclesiastes', *JSS* 3 (1958), pp. 336-43.

—'Koheleth's Use of Genesis', *JSS* 5 (1960), pp. 256-63.

Fox, M.V., 'The Meaning of *Hebel* for Qohelet', *JBL* 105 (1986), pp. 409-27.

—'Qohelet's Epistemology', *HUCA* 58 (1987), pp. 137-55.

—'Aging and Death in Qohelet 12', *JSOT* 42 (1988), pp. 55-77.

—'Qohelet 1.4', *JSOT* 40 (1988), p. 109.

—*Qohelet and his Contradictions* (JSOTSup, 71; Sheffield: JSOT Press, 1989).

Fredericks, D.C., *Qoheleth's Language: Re-evaluating its Nature and Date* (Lewiston, NY, 1988).

—'Chiasm and Parallel Structure in Qoheleth 5.9–6.9', *JBL* 108 (1989), pp. 17-35.

—'Life's Storms and Structural Unity in Qoheleth 11.1–12.8', *JSOT* 52 (1991), pp. 95-114.

Frendo, A., 'The "Broken Construct Chain" in Qoh 10.10b', *Bib* 62 (1981), pp. 544-45.

Galling, K., 'Kohelet-Studien', *ZAW* 50 (1932), pp. 276-99.

—'Stand und Aufgabe der Kohelet-Forschung', *ThR* 6 (1934), pp. 355-73.

—'Das Rätsel der Zeit im Urteil Kohelets (Koh 3, 1-15)', *ZTK* 58 (1961), pp. 1-12.

—*Der Prediger* (*HAT* I, 18; Tübingen, 1969).

Gese, H., 'The Crisis of Wisdom in Koheleth', pp. 141-53 in J.L. Crenshaw (ed.) *Theodicy in the Old Testament* (Philadelphia, 1983). Trans. from 'Die Krisis der Weisheit bei Koheleth', pp. 139-51, in F. Wendel (ed.), *Les sagesses du Proche-Orient ancient* (Paris, 1963).

Gilbert, M., 'La description de la vieillesse en Qohelet XII.7, est elle allégorique?' VTSup 32 (1981), pp. 96-109.

Ginsberg, H.L., *The Legend of King Keret* (New Haven, 1946).

—'The Structure and Contents of the Book of Koheleth', VTSup 3 (1955), pp. 138-49.

—*Koheleth* (Tel Aviv, 1961).

Ginsburg, C.D., *Coheleth or the Book of Ecclesiastes* (London, 1861).

Glasser, E., *Le procés du bonheur par Qohelet* (Paris, 1970).

Good, E.M., 'The Unfilled Sea: Style and Meaning in Ecclesiastes 1.2-11', pp. 59-73 in J.G. Gammie, *et al.* (eds.), *Israelite Wisdom* (Missoula, 1978).

—*Irony in the Old Testament* (Sheffield, 1981).

Goodman, A.E., 'The Words of Ahiquar', in D.W. Thomas (ed.), *Documents from Old Testament Times* (New York, 1961), pp. 270-75.

Gordis, R., 'Quotations as a Literary Usage in Biblical, Oriental and Rabbinic Literature', *HUCA* 22 (1949), pp. 157-219.

—*Koheleth—The Man and his World* (New York, 1968).

Gorssen, L., 'La cohérence de la conception de Dieu dans l'Ecclésiastes', *ETL* 46 (1970), pp. 282-324.

Haupt, P., *Ecclesiastes* (Baltimore, 1905).

Hengel, M., *Judaism and Hellenism* (Philadelphia, 1974).

Hertzberg, H.W., *Der Prediger* (*KAT* n.f. XVII, 4. Gütersloh, 1963).

Isaksson, B., *Studies in the Language of Qoheleth* (Uppsala, 1987).

Jaspar, F.N., 'Ecclesiastes: A Note for Our Time', *Int* 21 (1967), pp. 259-73.

Jenni, E., 'Das Wort *'ōlām* im Alten Testament', *ZAW* 65 (1953), pp. 1-35.

Johnston, R.K., ' "Confessions of a Workaholic": A Reappraisal of Qoheleth', *CBQ* 38 (1976), pp. 14-28.

Kaiser, O., *Der Mensch unter dem Schicksal* (Berling, 1985).

Kidner, D., *The Wisdom of Proverbs, Job, and Ecclesiastes* (Downers Grove, 1985).

Klopfenstein, M.A., 'Die Skepsis des Qohelet', *TZ* 28 (1972), pp. 97-109.

Knopf, C.S., 'The Optimism of Koheleth', *JBL* 49 (1930), pp. 195-99.

Koch, K., 'Is There a Doctrine of Retribution in the Old Testament?', in J.L. Crenshaw (ed.), *Theodicy in the Old Testament* (Philadelphia, 1983), pp. 57-87

Kugel, J.L., 'Qohelet and Money', *CBQ* 51 (1989), pp. 32-49.

Lambert, W.L., *Babylonian Wisdom Literature* (Oxford, 1975).

Lauha, A., 'Die Krise des religiönsen Glaubens bei Kohelet', VTSup 3 (1954), pp. 183-91.

—*Kohelet* (BKAT, 19; Neukirchen–Vluyn, 1978).

Leahy, M., 'The Meaning of Ecclesiastes 12:2-5', *ITQ* 19 (1952), pp. 297-300.

Levy, L., *Das Buch Qoheleth* (Leipzig, 1912).

Loader, J.A., 'Qoheleth 3.2-8—A "Sonnet" in the Old Testament', *ZAW* 81 (1969), pp. 240-42.

—*Polar Structures in the Book of Qoheleth* (BZAW, 152; Berlin, 1979).

—*Ecclesiastes* (Grand Rapids, 1986).

Lohfink, N., 'War Kohelet ein Frauenfiend? Ein Versuch die Logik und den Gegenstand von Qoh 7, 23–8.1a herauszufinden', in M. Gilbert (ed.), *La sagesse de l'Ancien Testament* (Gembloux, 1979), pp. 259-87.

—*Kohelet* (Wurzberg, 1980).

—'Die Wiederkehr des immer Gleichen! Eine frühe Synthese zwischen griechischen und jüdischem Weltgefühl in Kohelet 1.4-11', *Archivio di Filosophia* 53 (1985), pp. 125-49.

—'The Present and Eternity: Time in Qoheleth', *TD* 34 (1987), pp. 236-40. Trans. from 'Gegenwart und Ewigkeit: Die Zeit im Buch Kohelet', in *Geist und Leben* 60 (1987), pp. 2-12.

Loretz, D., *Qohelet und der Alte Orient* (Freiburg, 1964).

Lys, D., 'Par le temps qui court (Eccl 3.1-8)', *ETR* 48 (1973), pp. 299-316.

—*L'Ecclésiaste ou que vaut la vie?* (Paris, 1977).

—'L'être et le temps: communication de Qohèlèth', in M. Gilbert (ed.), *La sagesse de l'Ancien Testament* (Gembloux, 1979), pp. 249-58.

MacDonald, D.B., *The Hebrew Philosophical Genius: A Vindication* (Princeton, 1936).

McKane, W., *Proverbs: A New Approach* (Philadelphia, 1975).

Meek, T.J., 'Translating the Bible', *KBL* 79 (1960), pp. 328-35.

Michel, D., *Qohelet* (BZAW, 183; Berlin, 1989).

Mitchell, H.G., ' "Work" in Ecclesiastes', *JBL* 32 (1913), pp. 123-39.

Müller, H.P., 'Wie Sprachj Qohälät von Gott?', *VT* 18 (1968), pp. 507-21.

—'Neige der althebräischen "Weisheit": Zum Denken Qohäläts', *ZAW* 90 (1978), pp. 238-64.

—'Theonome Skepsis und Lebenfreude—zu Koh 1, 12–3, 15', *BZ* 30 (1986), pp. 1-19.

Murphy, R.E., 'The Interpretation of Old Testament Wisdom Literature', *Int* 23 (1969), pp. 289-301.

—'Qohelet's "Quarrel" with the Fathers', in D.Y. Hadidian (ed.), *From Faith to Faith* (Pittsburgh, 1979), pp. 235-45.

—'Qohelet Interpreted: The Bearing of the Past on the Future', *VT* 32 (1982), pp. 331-37.

Ogden, G.S., 'The "Better"-Proverb, Rhetorical Criticism, and Qoheleth', *JBL* 96 (1977), pp. 489-505.

—'Qoheleth's Use of the "Nothing is Better" Form', *JBL* 98 (1979), pp. 339-50.

—'Qoheleth XI 1-6', *VT* 33 (1983), pp. 222-30.

—'Qoheleth XI 7–II 8: Qoheleth's Summons to Enjoyment and Reflection', *VT* 34 (1984), pp. 27-38.

—'The Interpretation of *dôr* in Ecclesiastes 1.4', *JSOT* 34 (1986), pp. 91-92.

—*Qoheleth* (Sheffield, 1987).

—' "Vanity" it Certainly Is Not', *BT* 38 (1987), pp. 301-307.

—'Translation Problems in Ecclesiastes 5.13-17', *BT* 39 (1989), pp. 423-28.

Polk, T., 'The Wisdom of Irony: A Study of *Hebel* and its Relation to Joy and Fear of God in Ecclesiastes', *Studia Biblica et Theologica* 6 (1971), pp. 3-17.

Priest, J.F., 'Humanism, Skepticism, and Pessimism in Israel', *JAAR* 36 (1968), pp. 311-26.

Pritchard, J.B., *Ancient Near Eastern Texts Relating to the Old Testament* (Princeton, 1955).

Rad, G. von *Wisdom in Israel* (Nashville, 1972).

Rainey, A.F., 'A Second Look at "'āmal" in Qoheleth', *Concordia Theological Monthly* 36 (1965), p. 805.

Rankin, O.S., *Israel's Wisdom Literature* (Edinburgh, 1954).

Reines, C.W., 'Koheleth on Wisdom and Wealth', *JJS* 5 (1954), pp. 80-84.

Rosenthal, F., review of *The Legend of King Kerat*, by H.L. Ginsburg, *Or* 19 (1947), p. 402.

Rousseau, F., 'Structure de Qohélet i 4-11 et plan du livre', *VT* 31 (1981), pp. 200-17.

Rylaardsdam, J.C., *Revelation in Jewish Wisdom Literature* (Chicago, 1946).

Saiz, J.R.B., 'BWR'YK (Qoh. 12, 1) Reconsiderado', *Sef* 46 (1986), pp. 85-87.

Salters, R.B., 'A Note on the Exegesis of Ecclesiastes 3.15b', *ZAW* 88 (1976), pp. 419-22.

Savignac, J. de 'La sagesse du Qohéléth et l'epopee de Gilgamesh', *VT* 28 (1978), pp. 318-23.

Sawyer, J.F.A., 'The Ruined House in Ecclesiastes 12: A Reconstruction of the Original Parable', *JBL* 94 (1975), pp. 519-31.

Schmid, H.H., *Wesen und Geschichte der Weisheit* (BZAW, 101; Berlin, 1966).

Schoors, A., 'Kohelet: A Perspective of Life after Death?', *ETL* 61 (1985), pp. 295-303.

Scott, R.B.V., *Proverbs: Ecclesiastes* (New York, 1965).

Seybold, D', 'hebel', *TDOT* III.313-20 (Grand Rapids, 1978).

Staples, W.E., 'The "Vanity" of Ecclesiastes', *JNES* 2 (1943), pp. 95-104.

—' "Profit" in Ecclesiastes', *JNES* 4 (1945), pp. 87-96.

—'Vanity of Vanities', *Canadian Journal of Theology* 1 (1955), pp. 141-56.

—'Meaning of *hepes* in Ecclesiastes', *JNES* 24 (1965), pp. 110-12.

Toy, C.H., *The Book of Proverbs* (ICC, New York, 1902).

Waard, J. de 'The Translator and Textual Criticism (with particular reference to Eccl. 2.25', *Bib* 60 (1979), pp. 509-29.

Whitley, C.F., *Koheleth: His Language and Thought* (*BZAW*, 148; Berlin, 1976).

Whybray, R.N., 'Qoheleth the Immoralist? (Qoh 7.16-17)', in J.G. Gammie (ed.), *Israelite Wisdom* (Missoula, 1978), pp. 191-20.

—'Conservatisme et radicalisme dans Qohelet', in E. Jacobs (ed.), *Sagesse et religion* (Paris, 1979), pp. 65-91.

—'Qoheleth, Preacher of Joy', *JSOT* 23 (1982), pp. 87-98.

—'Ecclesiastes 1.5-7 and the Wonders of Nature', *JSOT* 41 (1988), pp. 105-12.

—*Ecclesiastes* (NCB, Grand Rapids, 1989).

Williams, J.G., 'What Does it Profit a Man?', *Judaism* 20 (1971), pp. 179-93.

Williams, R.J., 'Reflections on the *Lebensmüde*', *JEA* 48 (1962), pp. 49-56.

Witzenrath, H., *Süss ist das Licht: Eine literaturewissen schaftliche Untersuchung zu Koh 11, 7–12, 7* (St Ottilien, 1979).

Wright, A.G., 'The Riddle of the Sphinx: The Structure of the Book of Qoheleth', *CBQ* 30 (1968), pp. 313-34.

Zimmerli, W., *Das Buch des Predigers Salomo*, in *ATD* XVI (Göttingen, 1962), pp. 123-253.

—'The Place and Limit of the Wisdom in the Framework of the Old Testament Theology', *SJT* 17 (1964), pp. 146-58.

INDEXES

INDEX OF BIBLICAL REFERENCES

Coping with Transience

10.4	60	13.5	58	17.1	94
10.5	60	13.9	39	17.8	62
10.8	62	13.10	62	17.10	62
10.10	58	13.11	22	17.14	58
10.11	58	13.13	62	17.19	58
10.12	62	13.14	58	17.20	58
10.13	58	13.18	62	17.23	62
10.16	39	13.22	85, 87	17.27	58
10.17	62	13.23	79	17.28	58
10.18	58	14.3	58	18.2	58
10.19	58	14.4	63	18.4	58
10.20	58	14.5	58	18.6	58
10.21	58	14.7	58	18.7	58
10.25	39, 85	14.11	85	18.8	58
10.26	60	14.16	62	18.9	60
10.27	39, 85	14.17	62	18.13	58
10.31	58	14.23	60	18.20	58
10.32	58	14.25	58	18.21	58
11.4	39	14.29	62	18.22	63, 68
11.5	85	14.32	39, 85	18.23	79
11.9	58	14.35	61, 63	19.5	58
11.11	58	15.1	58, 62,	19.9	58
11.12	58		82	19.10	80
11.13	58	15.2	58	19.12	63
11.19	39	15.4	58	19.14	63, 68
11.30	39	15.7	58	19.15	60
12.1	62	15.12	62	19.16	39
12.4	63, 68	15.19	60	19.19	62
12.6	58	15.22	62	19.20	62
12.7	85	15.23	58	19.21	57
12.11	28, 60	15.27	62	19.24	60
12.13	58	15.28	58	19.25	62
12.14	58	15.31	62	19.27	62
12.15	62	15.32	62	20.1	63
12.16	63	16.3	56	20.2	63
12.17	58	16.4	38, 56	20.3	58
12.18	58	16.8	94	20.4	60
12.19	58	16.12	61	20.8	61
12.20	58	16.13-15	63	20.13	60
12.22	58	16.20	62	20.15	58
12.23	58	16.21	58	20.18	62
12.24	60	16.23	58	20.25	58
12.25	58	16.24	58	20.26	61
12.27	60	16.26	60	21.5	60
12.28	39	16.27	58	21.6	19, 22
13.2	58	16.28	58	21.11	62
13.3	58	16.30	58	21.14	62
13.4	60	16.32	62	21.17	63

2.11	12, 29, 52, 75, 76, 93		66, 85, 87, 90, 93	4.1-3	33, 45
2.12-14	74	3.1-8	24, 27, 37, 56, 69	4.1	26, 40, 80
2.12-26	37			4.2	35, 40
2.12	14, 25, 26, 46, 55, 80	3.1-22	43	4.3	35
		3.1	38, 95	4.4-8	93
2.13	35, 49, 53	3.2-8	57	4.4	12, 29, 49, 50, 59, 80, 93
		3.2	34, 37, 38, 45, 57		
2.14-23	75, 76			4.5	60, 80
2.14-16	53			4.6	29, 60, 67, 93
2.14	35, 80	3.4	64, 68, 69, 80	4.7-12	59
2.15	12, 54, 76, 93	3.5	68, 69	4.7	12, 26, 59, 60, 93, 94
2.16	14, 35, 54, 76, 81	3.7	58		
		3.8	68, 69, 80	4.8	12, 31, 51, 59, 60, 66, 93, 94
2.17	12, 29, 53, 79, 93	3.9	49, 51		
		3.11	14, 27, 38, 73, 93	4.9	50
2.18-23	46			4.12	82
2.18-21	20	3.12	51, 66, 75, 88	4.13-16	76
2.18	25, 45, 53, 55, 79, 81, 87	3.13	51, 52, 66, 67, 75	4.13	50, 61, 80
				4.14	35
				4.15	25
2.19	12, 45, 47, 55, 81, 93	3.14	14, 37, 46, 57, 73, 82, 91	4.16	12, 29, 93
				5.1-6	87, 88
2.20	51, 53	3.15	26, 56	5.1-7	58, 60
2.21	12, 29, 31, 51, 87, 93	3.16	80, 85, 86	5.1	80, 87, 88
		3.17	36, 37, 85, 86, 88, 95	5.3	46, 58, 80, 95
2.22-25	51				
2.22-26	52, 64	3.18-22	57	5.4	50
2.22	49, 67	3.18	36	5.5	50, 58
2.23	12, 14, 29, 48, 79, 93	3.19-21	53	5.6	87
		3.19-22	64	5.7	12, 15, 24, 46, 80, 93
2.24-26	46, 75, 76	3.19	12, 29, 36, 92	5.8	60, 61, 61, 82
2.24	52, 53, 65, 67	3.20	25, 34, 36	5.9–6.9	42, 43, 49, 60, 69, 71, 73, 74, 93
2.25	14, 53, 65, 66	3.21	47		
2.26	12, 20, 29, 52,	3.22	14, 46, 51, 53, 66, 67		

INDEX OF AUTHORS